HOW TO LIBERATE
THE WORLD IN 30 DAYS

Become a "Certified Liberty Instructor!"
This devotional book is part of our easy, self-paced
30-lesson curriculum that we will license you to teach
your local small groups. Get credit by simply e-mailing us
one short essay after each chapter. Then access our videos
to show your class by joining our private, members-only
mentoring group: http://SchoolOfLiberty.org

SchoolOfLiberty.org

To order multiple copies or boxes of this book at a
bulk discount, call us toll-free at
1-866-Obey-God.

HOW TO LIBERATE
THE WORLD IN 30 DAYS

A Step-by-Step Guide to Take Back Your Country

by

CHAPLAIN GORDON JAMES KLINGENSCHMITT, PHD

HOW TO LIBERATE
THE WORLD IN 30 DAYS

World Ahead Press is a division of WND Books. The views and opinions expressed in this book are those of the author and do not necessarily reflect the official policy or position or WND Books.

Paperback ISBN: 978-1-946918-00-0
eBook ISBN: 978-1-946918-01-7

Printed in the United States of America
16 17 18 19 20 21 XXX 9 8 7 6 5 4 3 2 1

CONTENTS

FOREWORD
BY DR. ALAN KEYES

True liberty does not depend on the support of government. Rather, just government derives its powers from the good will of those who join in the pursuit of right, by God instructed and endowed. In making the Revolution that gave birth to our nation the people of the United States exercised just such powers. In due course, they established a Constitution of government framed to use them continually to secure their exercise of God-endowed rights, including liberty. Christian faith is, and has ever been, the key support for America's liberty. Without it our Constitution would never have been conceived, nor long endured.

Chaplain, activist, PhD, and legislator Gordon Klingenschmitt's life exemplifies this fact. In the present crisis of our existence as a free people, his right-spirited courage, like that of Christian pastors throughout our history, represents the true mind of American liberty. Derived from his personal experience, this manual for Christian citizenship equips others to do likewise. Step by step it lays out a path of confident activism, by which people of good faith can act as the wholesome leaven by which the self-government of the American people rises to be, once again, the occasion of God's blessings upon us and our posterity.

INTRODUCTION

"It is for freedom that Christ has set us free. Stand firm, then, and do not let yourselves be burdened again by a yoke of slavery" (Gal. 5:1).

In thirty days, you can liberate the world. I say liberate, not rule, because Christ is already King, so we need not lust for power. But sadly, our fallen world is under bondage to sin, ruled by a spiritual adversary, and in need of liberation from tyrannical dictators.

Evil controls most political systems, governments, and newspapers, but when the enemy comes in like a flood, God raises up a standard. You are the standard!

This book is many things: A game plan, a blueprint, a method, a guideline, a prayer devotional, a course curriculum, and a primer for the politically curious. I pray it sparks a wildfire. It has been my experience that where the devil tries to stamp out Jesus' name, Jesus spreads like wildfire among His people. It is my intention with this book to spark that wildfire, first in your mind, and eventually liberating the entire world for Christ.

It's a primer consisting of thirty short devotions to be read daily in thirty days, with fifteen true stories of political victory that will inspire you to see what is possible. It may take you a lifetime to liberate the world for Christ, but what better cause exists?

Share this book with your team, your church, your pastor, your fellow politicos, and especially every young person you know. Master these thirty tools by practicing them over time. They really work. You really can save the world, or at least your corner of it.

God bless you as you restore liberty and take back your country.

VICTORY STORY

NAVY CHAPLAIN TAKES
A STAND FOR JESUS

I'm an Air Force Academy graduate, promoted to USAF Major, but I volunteered for a pay cut, demotion and switched to the Navy to become a chaplain. Serving aboard U.S.S. ANZIO in Operation Iraqi Freedom, I preached on Sundays at sea, led forty-five Sailors to Christ, and my Sailors won six awards for community service, including best in Navy, because Fridays ashore we fed the homeless. I defended my Jewish Sailor's right to eat Kosher food, my Muslim Sailor's right to pray to Allah, and I even invited atheists to come teach our Bible study group.

But I was inspired by the Holy Bible and Charles Finney's *Lectures on Revival,* so I prayed daily for Christian revival. I fasted many days. I wanted to save souls, not just on my ship, but in the whole fleet, Navy, and America. One day in prayer, I sensed the Lord saying, "You're always praying for revival, but are you willing to pay the price?"

I answered, "Yes, Lord, I'd even give up my career, please just give me a nation-wide revival for America to stand for Jesus Christ." I sensed God reply, "We have a deal." So I predicted to my roommate I'd soon lose my career but spark a national revival.

Months later that prophetic word began to come true. One of my Sailors died, tragically, in a motorcycle wreck. My commander asked me to preach at a Christian memorial service honoring my dead Sailor's faith, in the Norfolk base chapel. Attendance was optional. The law clearly permits chaplains to preach the gospel in church, so I did.

"I have good news," I preached. "Our friend is in heaven today." I quoted John 3:36: "Whoever believes in the Son, he has eternal life, but whoever rejects the Son will not see life, for God's wrath remains on them." My CO got mad and called me to his office.

"I heard you say Jesus is the only way to heaven," said the ship's Captain. "Were you telling me I must accept Jesus Christ?" he asked. Of course, I had never mentioned him, but he punished me in writing three times for that one sermon and told a Navy board to end my career because I quoted the Bible in church, overemphasizing Jesus in a sermon.

He broke the law that protects chaplains' rights, but the Navy investigators swept it under the carpet. So I called a Christian lawyer who said sixty-five other chaplains were suing the Navy. All were denied promotion because they prayed and preached in Jesus' name. "Do you know any Congressmen?" he asked me.

My bachelor's degree is in political science, but how can one man take on the Pentagon and wake up the entire US Congress? To awaken Congress, you need phone calls by citizens. To wake up citizens, you need the press to tell your story. To get reporters, you need to be a whistleblower. So I did something crazy.

I staged an eighteen-day hunger strike in front of the White House. I lost fourteen pounds, but my story landed on the front pages of the *Washington Post, Washington Times,* and the *New York Times.*

Quickly the revival began. Thousands of citizens stood with me for Christ. Phones in DC rang off the hook, and seventy-five Congressmen and Senators wrote to the President on my behalf. The Navy brass backpedaled and surrendered, renewing my contract for three years. We won, for the time being. My career was saved, but the Navy brass were mad as hornets, and the national revival that God had promised me was just beginning.

*Former Navy Chaplain Gordon Klingenschmitt prays
in front of the White House*

DAY 1

TOOL: RIGHT MOTIVES WHY DO YOU WANT TO LIBERATE THE WORLD?

Christians must not seek to rule the world for self, but to liberate it from the rule of evil. Totalitarian sin controls us. The devil tyrannically rules many hearts. *But Jesus is the original libertarian.* He is our rescuer, a knight in shining armor who breaks our chains from the law (rulership) of sin. When His Spirit of Liberty frees our hearts from evil, we resist tyranny.

"Don't you know that when you offer yourselves to someone as obedient slaves, you are slaves of the one you obey—whether you are slaves to sin, which leads to death, or to obedience, which leads to righteousness?" (Rom. 6:16). Having been freed by Christ, why would you allow your political world, your family, your children, your country, to be ruled by evildoers? "It is for freedom that Christ has set us free. Stand firm, then, and do not let yourselves be burdened again by a yoke of slavery" (Gal. 5:1).

This is why Christians run for political office: to preserve our personal liberty from the evil one and evildoers. We seek to love God and neighbor rather than self, and we "do nothing out of selfish ambition or vain conceit. Rather, in humility value others above yourselves" (Phil. 2:3). We seek not to proudly rule, but to humbly serve. We worship God, not power. We are servant leaders because Christ served us.

When Lucifer served as a worship-leading angel, he was tempted to receive worship for himself and fell into pride and sin. He arrogantly thought he could rule better than God, so he rebelled. Later, Satan tempted Christ with worldly power, but Jesus replied, "Worship the Lord your God, and serve him only" (Matt. 4:10). Through humble resistance to sin, Christ the King took power back.

God commands us to rule this world. "Let us make mankind in our image, in our likeness, **so that they may rule** . . . over all the creatures" (Gen. 1:26.) "**Occupy** till I come" (Luke 19:13, KJV) was Christ's command in the parable of the talents. "A Republic, if you can **keep it,**" said Ben Franklin to Mrs. Elizabeth Powel.

You were created **so that you may rule** your corner of the earth, and **occupy**, and **keep it**. It's why God liberated you, so you may liberate others. Maybe you'll never be President. But you could be mayor of a small town, or gently govern your home and kids. If Christ rules you, then loves rules you. Now go and love the world.

Self-government is our mandate. "The fruit of the Spirit is . . . self-control. Against such things there is no law" (Gal. 5:22–24). Now let's liberate the world.

Pray this prayer: *"Father in heaven, I repent of all pride and selfish ambition. I don't want to establish my own kingdom, but yours. Rule in my heart first. Liberate me from sin and selfishness; then let me build your kingdom with love, so I may liberate others to worship and obey you, not me. In Jesus' name, amen."*

Assignment: *Self examine to get rid of selfish motives. Desire to liberate, not just rule.*

Get Credit: *Write 25 to 40 words engaging with ideas in this chapter and e-mail them to* homework@schoolofliberty.org *under the email subject "Liberate Chapter 1."*

If you engage with all 30 chapters, we'll make you a "Certified Liberty Instructor." You might earn pay. Visit http://SchoolOfLiberty.org to learn more.

WRITE YOUR PERSONAL NOTES AND QUESTIONS BELOW:

DAY 2

TOOL: RIGHT VECTOR
LEADERSHIP TOWARD GOOD, NOT EVIL

At the U.S. Air Force Academy where I earned my bachelors in political science, they taught me the meaning of leadership. We learned character, integrity, service, excellence, and we lived up to an honor code, making service to our nation higher than self.

Although I served twenty-plus years in the military, I thank God that our country is not ruled by force by military dictators, but by elected officials who rule by our consent through elections. Democracies never go to war against other democracies, so as all dictators disappear, Lord willing, only those who win elections will write future laws. This means in order to legislate or liberate, we must win elections.

As a Christian political activist who has helped change bad policies in thirteen states and won election to the Colorado State House of Representatives (and later lost a primary race for State Senate), I learned that liberating the world begins with liberating yourself. You must examine your own heart to remove character flaws if you want to rule well, that is, if you want to move the world toward good, not evil.

Let's imagine you run for office and eventually win. There you are, on top of the world, in charge, making or enforcing laws that others must obey. If you are full of evil, the people you govern will groan under the weight of your oppression. "When the righteous thrive, the people rejoice; when the wicked rule, the people groan" (Prov. 29:2).

It is critical, therefore, that you become a morally good person. Building character takes years, but it begins with taking a fearless moral inventory of all that is wrong inside of you. Will you cheat to win? Will you lie? Will you steal? Do the ends justify the means?

History is replete with examples of powerful but immoral leaders: Stalin, Hitler, Mao, Ceausescu, Hussein, and someday the Antichrist himself will clench his fist of tyranny to eliminate all who are good.

Don't step on others to climb your ladder. Compare them to Jesus Christ, who laid down His life, sacrificed his own right to rule, and "took one for the team" because His cause was greater than self. The greatest leaders of our generation—saints like Mother Teresa, political leaders like Gandhi, or activists like Martin Luther King Jr. or Rosa Parks—selflessly led their generation toward good, not evil.

"A dispute also arose among them as to which of them was considered to be greatest. Jesus said to them, 'The kings of the Gentiles lord it over them; and those who exercise authority over them call themselves Benefactors. But you are not to be like that. Instead, the greatest among you should be like the youngest, and the one who rules like the one who serves'" (Luke 22:24–26). Become a servant leader.

Pray this prayer: *"Father in heaven, help me clearly discern good from evil, first within my own heart and then in the world around me, so that when I succeed and become a servant leader, I will only lead others toward good, never evil. In Jesus' name, amen."*

Assignment: *Examine yourself first so that you can lead others toward holiness and good, not sin and evil.*

Get Credit: *Write 25 to 40 words engaging with ideas in this chapter and e-mail them to* homework@ schoolofliberty.org *under the e-mail subject "Liberate Chapter 2."*

If you engage with all 30 chapters, we'll make you a "Certified Liberty Instructor." You might earn pay. Visit http://SchoolOfLiberty.org to learn more.

WRITE YOUR PERSONAL NOTES AND QUTESTIONS BELOW:

VICTORY STORY

COURT-MARTIAL, VINDICATED BY CONGRESS

Six weeks after the Navy renewed my contract, the Admirals and senior chaplains were angry with me. I had caused a stir, so they conspired to get rid of the whistleblower.

The top chaplain, a liberal anti-Jesus two-star Admiral, wrote a bad new policy and fooled the Secretary of the Navy into signing it. SECNAVINST 1730.7C authorized commanders to punish chaplains if they prayed "in Jesus' name" outside of Sunday chapel. It required nonsectarian prayers. In other words, it was okay to pray to God and say amen, but chaplains couldn't say the "J" word in public without punishment.

My supervisor explained the policy, saying "Chaplain Klingenschmitt, will you go pray at this? Yes. Are you going to pray in Jesus' name? Yes. You can't go. If you do go, and you do pray in Jesus' name, you can be punished. Because it is the CO's call."

What would you do? I prayed for guidance and remembered Peter and John in Acts. The Pharisees "commanded them not to speak or teach at all in the name of Jesus. But Peter and John replied, 'Which is right in God's eyes: to listen to you, or to him? You be the judges!'" (Acts 4:18–19). They disobeyed men, but obeyed God. They were flogged.

So I did another crazy thing. I disobeyed the policy. I called my friend from Alabama, Judge Roy Moore, and together we stood in front of the White House. On a Thursday morning I wore my Navy uniform and prayed "in Jesus' name" on national television.

The Navy brass offered to punish me quietly with a piece of paper in my record. I refused and demanded my right to a trial in court. "It's a misdemeanor," they pleaded, "take the paper quietly and you can keep your career and pension." Instead I fell on my sword and demanded my own court-martial.

Even though the Navy judge admitted uniform regulations allowed chaplains to pray in uniform, he enforced 1730.7C instead. He ruled that "public worship" was defined by Congress as legal, but only in Sunday chapel. Under the new policy "worshiping in public" was illegal in uniform outside of Sunday chapel. I was found **guilty of worshiping in public,** disobeying "lawful" orders, and violating the new Navy policy.[1]

After my crucifixion came a resurrection. My "guilty" verdict was published in five hundred newspapers that week. Led by thirty-five pro-family political groups, three hundred thousand Americans petitioned Congress. *God answered our prayers and gave America a true revival.*

National TV and radio hosts interviewed me daily, and I met the chief of staff for the top U.S. Senator of the Senate Armed Services Committee. The day after that meeting, the senator spoke on the floor of the U.S. Senate: "I am being besieged by telephone, by bloggers, by everything else. . . I am basically assured by the Department of Defense that they will comply; stay for the time being the most recent regulations . . . SECNAVINST 1730.7C." [2]

Congress ordered the Navy to rescind that policy. The naval secretary repented and reversed the policy, restoring freedom for other chaplains to pray "in Jesus' name." We won, but I was involuntarily and honorably discharged. I lost my sixteen-year officer career, and lost a million-dollar pension. Was it worth it? Yes, I kept my soul.

Chaps in DC meeting with Congressmen Conaway, McIntyre,
Jones, and Franks

DAY 3

TOOL: RIGHT SPIRIT
PRAYER IS FIRST STEP, LAST STEP,
EVERY STEP

"Unless the LORD builds the house,
the builders labor in vain" (Psalm 127:1).

When you first realize that ruling the world means establishing God's kingdom of good on earth, not your selfish kingdom of evil, pride, and ambition, you'll also realize you have a great Ally on your side, for God already rules in heaven. That is good news.

The God of the Bible wants His divine will to be done on earth now, in our lifetime. His will is not always done on earth. We don't always win, and God's kingdom has yet to be established. In the end it will be, but today we have much work to do. Remember, God is with us now, if we partner with Him to bring about His will in our world.

Muslims believe fatalistically that all historic events must have been the will of Allah, including evil events. But

Christians are not fatalistic or powerless, and we are called to establish love and good, and triumph over selfishness and evil. We believe God wants us to build His Kingdom of love blessing, healing, compassion, life, and conquer our invisible adversary the devil who wants suffering, cursing, and death. Our God is not the author of evil, but he allows it so that we may be trained to overcome it.

Hence the need for prayer, which helps us partner with God to bring about His will and kingdom, and defeat the devil's will and kingdom. Prayer invites God into our world, so God answers by showing up with blessing and life. Without prayer we build bricks without straw. Without God all our kingdom building is selfish, meaningless vanity. Asking God for His kingdom is the first step, the last step, and every step in your political conquest. James says, "You do not have because you do not ask God" (James 4:2). We are commanded to take dominion (see Gen. 1:28), but not for self, so we must invite the Holy Spirit to invade our hearts and cleanse us from evil. It's God's kingdom. He is real. He is here. He will guide us and change us. He will inspire others. He will take dominion on this earth, but we must humbly ask Him or He will use others instead of us.

God withholds His blessing until we ask: "Thus saith the Lord GOD; I will yet for this be enquired of by the house of Israel, to do it for them; I will increase them with men like a flock" (Ez. 36:37, KJV). He will not increase our flock until we enquire in prayer.

God does nothing without showing us in prayer: "The Sovereign LORD does nothing without revealing his plan to his servants the prophets" (Amos 3:7).

Joshua learned this before conquering Jericho. He asked the angel, "Are you for us or for our enemies?" But that angel was Christ. " 'Neither,' he replied, 'but as commander of the army of the LORD I have now come.' Then Joshua fell facedown to the ground in reverence" (Joshua 5:13–14). We are merely soldiers.

Remember *you* are not creating a new movement alone, you are joining God's plan that is already in place and unfolding. God's kingdom already grows in the hearts of other Christian activists. Join us and pray with us.

Pray this prayer: *"Father in heaven, I pray Your kingdom come, Your will be done, on earth as it is in heaven. Establish your will in our world, now. In Jesus' name, amen."*

Assignment: *Commit to a life of prayer. Pray first, last, and every step of the battle.*

Get Credit: *Write 25 to 40 words engaging with ideas in this chapter and e-mail them to* homework@schoolofliberty.org *under the e-mail subject "Liberate Chapter 3."*

If you engage with all 30 chapters, we'll make you a "Certified Liberty Instructor." You might earn pay. Visit http://SchoolOfLiberty.org to learn more.

WRITE YOUR PERSONAL NOTES AND QUESTIONS BELOW:

TOOL: RIGHT CAUSE
IDENTIFY A CAUSE WORTH DYING FOR

Many people in the world go many directions. Most are busy trying to find shelter, love, laughter, work, and feed their families. Most people do not pay attention to politics until politicians try to invade their lives, take away their freedoms, raise their taxes, or violate them with injustice. Then suddenly people wake up and pay attention. Sometimes when people see injustice done to others they get involved in politics. Maybe this is you. Maybe you're waking up.

What is the cause that got you hooked? Why are you reading this book? Why do you want to liberate the world? Chances are, you have seen something wrong or have been wronged. You want to fix it. Good. Let that motivation burn inside your soul. Remember the injustice you saw or experienced. Visualize your cause. Now fight to fix it. Make it right.

For me, it was religious freedom. When the government told me, a Navy chaplain, that I would be punished if I prayed in Jesus' name, something broke inside of me. The government's tyranny made me an activist. It changed my career and my life's calling. I demanded freedom, went on a hunger strike, demanded a court-martial, helped mobilize three hundred thousand petitioners, got seventy-five congressmen to write the President, and we changed the law. We restored freedom, but it cost my career. So I found a different calling. I've now gathered and sent five million petitions, helped change bad policies in thirteen states, and won an election. Religious liberty is the cause I'd die for.

For you it may be protecting your own children or ending world hunger and sickness, ending some injustice, or some other truly compassionate cause that makes you weep—or makes you angry. Good for you.

I'm not talking about personalities. If you wanted to follow Donald Trump or Hillary Clinton for their charismatic personalities, go for it. But most of us look deeper at the causes they claim to represent. What would drive millions of otherwise busy Americans to sacrifice their time, talent, and treasure to vote, donate, volunteer, or get politically involved? It's the cause, not just the person. For many Democrats, it's the injustice of social inequality. For liberty-minded Republicans, it's government intrusion preventing growth and opportunity. For Christians, we see evil in the world, and we want to replace it with goodness.

It's the cause, the cause, the cause people die for. If you find a godly cause, you can raise a political army and take over the world. People will follow you to hell and back if they believe your cause is theirs. They'll gladly give their lives, walk for hours knocking on doors for your campaign, open their wallets to help you succeed, sacrifice to help you win, because when you win, their cause wins and evil is conquered.

Pray this prayer: *"Father in heaven, give me the vision to see injustice the same way you see it and the motivation to fight passionately for your cause. In Jesus' name, amen."*

Assignment: *Name one godly cause you'd gladly die for. Say it. Write it down. Now commit your life to it.*

Get Credit: *Write 25 to 40 words engaging with ideas in this chapter and e-mail them to* homework@ schoolofliberty.org *under the email subject "Liberate Chapter 4."*

If you engage with all 30 chapters, we'll make you a "Certified Liberty Instructor." You might earn pay. Visit http://SchoolOfLiberty.org to learn more.

WRITE YOUR PERSONAL NOTES AND QUESTIONS BELOW:

VICTORY STORY

HOSPITAL CHAPLAIN TAKES A STAND

About a year after my honorable discharge, I read about a hospital chaplain in Florida named Danny Harvey. The hospital threatened him in writing that if he didn't stop praying "in Jesus' name," he'd be fired. I knew immediately how to help him.

First I verified his documents were true. Then I asked him what he wanted to do and if I could help.

"I'm a fourth generation Baptist preacher," Chaplain Harvey told me. "And Colossians 3:17 tells me 'whatever you do, whether in word or deed, do it all in the name of the Lord Jesus.' I cannot deny my Lord and Savior just to keep a job."

He informed the hospital that he'd continue to pray in Jesus' name, and Danny Harvey was fired the next day. What great political courage it takes to do the right thing when you know it will cost you dearly! Danny made Jesus proud by taking a stand. But it didn't end there.

Armed with a little publicity experience, I flew to Florida and issued press releases. We appeared together on Fox News and called for a public rally. Chaplain Harvey's local church pastor called other churches, and thirty congregations mobilized to attend the rally together. Twelve hundred people marched around the giant hospital building in silent protest that next Saturday. We wore matching T-shirts that say "My Jesus, my stand."

Any time you get thirty churches to agree on anything, that's a miracle. For twelve hundred citizens to attend a prayer rally together, that's a revival! Florida's Christian rally standing up for Chaplain Harvey's right to pray in Jesus' name made national news.

The hospital CEO's anti-Jesus behavior was exposed. He resigned that week and moved out of state in the face of public scandal. The board likely would have fired him, had he not resigned. The hospital issued an apology in the newspaper, saying it was okay to pray in Jesus' name in their hospital.

It was a victory for the Kingdom, but my friend, Chaplain Danny Harvey, the hero of the story, he never did get his hospital job back. He had served there eight years and prayed for countless patients in Jesus' name. His termination was the cost of godly obedience in the face of an ungodly policy. He obeyed God. He kept his soul. Jesus tells him to "rejoice and be glad, because great is your reward in heaven, for in the same way they persecuted the prophets who were before you" (Matt. 5:12).

" 'Truly I tell you,' Jesus replied, 'no one who has left home or brothers or sisters or mother or father or children or fields for me and the gospel will fail to receive a hundred times as much in this present age: homes, brothers, sisters, mothers, children and fields—along with persecutions—and in the age to come eternal life' " (Mark 10:29–30).

Danny and his family may be poor materially now, but they are rich beyond words in the spiritual world. Are you?

Twelve hundred citizens march for liberty with Chaplain Danny Harvey in Florida

TOOL: SPECIFIC GOALS
VISUALIZE THE LAWS YOU WANT PASSED

For most of human history, people were ruled by laws made by one or a few people in charge. Historically, laws were written by kings, however benevolent or tyrannical, who used military force to make others pay taxes and obey authoritarian edicts.

In America, in theory, that system has been reversed. It is now the citizens who rule their elected officials and hold them accountable through their votes and activism. Today, laws and even tax rates are written by *you*, or at least with your consent by proxy through those who represent you. Did you know that *you* write the laws? Or you should be writing them. And you can write laws, and lessen tyranny, if you *just get involved.*

Before I tell you how, I want you to visualize your cause. What is the injustice that angered you or the compassionate love that burns in your soul? What law, if written, would make your solution mandatory? Hopefully it aligns with the greatest law:

On one occasion an expert in the law stood up to test Jesus. "Teacher," he asked, "what must I do to inherit eternal life?" "What is written in the law?" he replied. "How do you read it?"

He answered, " 'Love the Lord your God with all your heart and with all your soul and with all your strength and with all your mind.'; and 'Love your neighbor as yourself.' "

"You have answered correctly," Jesus replied. "Do this and you will live." (Luke 10:26–28)

I believe all other laws should be based on this one law: Love God and love your neighbor. God wrote this law and will judge or reward our eternal life based on our obedience to it. As a Christian activist trying to implement God's law into our American system, I must work daily with all three branches established in our Constitution: the legislative, executive, and judicial branches that write, enforce, and judge the laws in America. The best place to start implementing change for good is at the local level.

Do you know your elected officials' names? Do you pray for them? Have you taken them out for coffee? Most locally elected officials are highly accessible. Find their office and schedule a meeting. Get to know them. They're reasonable people. Ask them how you can help them write a law that will fix your problem. They'll either tell you how to do it or become your obstacle, but either one is better than just ignoring you. If they tell you how to write a law, draft that law and put it in writing for them on their desk.

You don't need to be a lawyer—although lawyers are often involved—to write a law. I've written or helped pass or block laws long before I got elected. Citizens should write laws in collaboration with officials. If citizens do not do this collaboratively, then bad laws will be passed without your consent or awareness, and tyranny will defeat liberty. Wouldn't you rather get involved, and help liberate the world?

Prayer this prayer: *"Father in heaven, you are the ultimate King, Lawmaker, and Judge. Give me your divine wisdom to create a practical law for my community that you would want passed by human government here on earth. Then give me the courage and favor to work with elected officials to see it passed. In Jesus' name, amen."*

Assignment: *Write an informal idea you want in law. Then show it to your local official.*

Get Credit: *Write 25 to 40 words engaging with ideas in this chapter and e-mail them to* homework@ schoolofliberty.org *under the email subject "Liberate Chapter 5."*

If you engage with all 30 chapters, we'll make you a "Certified Liberty Instructor." You might earn pay. Visit http://SchoolOfLiberty.org to learn more.

WRITE YOUR PERSONAL NOTES AND QUESTIONS BELOW:

DAY 6

TOOL: GET SKILLS
GET AN EDUCATION, BUILD A RÉSUMÉ

Here's a hard reality: Selfless and loving Christians are called to liberate the world from many unethical or selfish people who also want to rule the world. Power is like a competitive sport. Your competitors, some who may hate your cause, are often smart, rich, handsome, articulate, and don't want you to win. Politics may look or feel dirty or bloody, but the good news is, you will soon find many friends willing to fight with you for your cause. God wants His kingdom built on earth. Even if you feel like you're alone, as the saying goes, "one person plus God makes a majority." You were made for this!

Have realistic expectations. You may not become President, so you may never need his or her college degrees or résumé. But the task before you does require you to have somewhat of a political education. I'm not talking about a four-year political science degree. I earned one; it looks nice on my wall, but I didn't need that to win office. I'm not talking about a law degree either. I'm not a lawyer, but I've learned to surround myself with excellent lawyers that can coach me to do the rest. Most U.S. Congressmen are not lawyers, but they hire them. Having any college or trade school degree is just as useful, honestly. Go to college; I encourage that, even if you're old. It doesn't matter your age; it's not too late to learn, and there are plenty of funding sources out there. But if you can't, you can still become political literate.

When I say get an education and build your résumé, I mean attend some three-day political seminars or take some webinars online or audit a community college class. You can also volunteer as an intern and learn by experience, which is the best teacher.

My four years in college did not fully prepare me for the whirlwind of real life politics. I had to learn on the fly when my cause took flight and suddenly I was on Capitol Hill meeting congressmen and showing them the scars of my injustice. Since then I have discovered a wealth of short-term classes, just three days each. Experts who had spent time in the trenches taught me real political activism skills, without textbooks. Here are some options:

- Register to see the online videos for this book. Go to: http://SchoolOfLiberty.org.

- Leadership Institute (LI) founder Morton Blackwell hosts you in DC for half-week seminars on twenty different topics fitting all your political campaign training needs. Go to: http://LeadershipInstitute.org.

- Center for Self Governance (CSG) comes to your location and will train teams to take back your local government. Go to: http://centerforselfgovernance.com.

- Foundation for Applied Conservative Leadership (FACL) comes to your location to train and motivate your team. Go to: http://facl-training.org.

- Your local county political party trains activists to help run their campaigns. Just show up and work, and learn by doing. That's the best method.

Pray this prayer: *"Father in heaven, I need knowledge to do the great things you've called me to do. Help me invest in my own political knowledge so I can win, and achieve actual success by using the knowledge you will give me. In Jesus' name, amen."*

Assignment: *Explore the sites listed above and sign up for any three-day class offered.*

<u>Get Credit</u>: *Write 25 to 40 words engaging with ideas in this chapter and e-mail them to* homework@ schoolofliberty.org *under the email subject "Liberate Chapter 6."*

If you engage with all 30 chapters, we'll make you a "Certified Liberty Instructor." You might earn pay. Visit http://SchoolOfLiberty.org to learn more.

WRITE YOUR PERSONAL NOTES AND QUESTIONS BELOW:

VICTORY STORY

SIX POLICE CHAPLAINS
RISK EVERYTHING

About a year after the hospital chaplain in Florida lost his job but kept his soul, six police chaplains in Virginia took a similar stand for Jesus. Seventeen Virginia state troopers, all chaplains, were called before their police superintendent and given strict orders to stop praying "in Jesus' name" at public ceremonies. They could pray to God but not to Jesus, they were told, or they would be de-frocked or fired.

Six of the seventeen chaplains immediately resigned in protest. They are heroes who took a stand for Christ rather than deny his name. They are Bible-believing evangelical Christians, here in America, who were forced to choose between Christ or government. They chose Jesus, who said "Whoever is ashamed of me and my words, the Son of Man will be ashamed of them when he comes in his glory and in the glory of the Father and of the holy angels" (Luke 9:26).

My friends at American Family Association and I got eighty-five Virginia pastors to sign a letter to Virginia

Governor Tim Kaine. He wrote back a three-page letter refusing to overrule his trooper superintendent or let any chaplains pray publicly "in Jesus' name." I gave his letter to the press, but he doubled down, stating publicly on television, "when I pray to God or the Lord I do that without mentioning Jesus," so must his chaplains.

So I organized a rally outside the governor's mansion. We advertised on the radio and a thousand Christians attended to stand up for Jesus and the chaplains. Two chaplain heroes attended, and several pastors and state legislators. The story had legs and public outrage was on our side, so our legislator friends introduced a pro-freedom bill.

The bill passed the state house on a mostly party-line vote, but it was blocked in the state senate by one anti-Jesus Democrat. He ran for governor on an anti-liberty platform. We then approached the Republican candidate Bob McDonnell, a fellow Regent graduate, who pledged to restore the chaplains' freedom if elected.

In the upcoming election cycle, we printed voter guides and faxed them to twenty-five hundred pastors across the entire commonwealth. We listed the pro-Jesus and anti-Jesus candidates, not just for governor but also listed the names of every anti-Jesus state legislator who voted against the bill for chaplains' rights.

Before our faxes went out, the polls showed 43 percent to 41 percent for the Republican, but six weeks later, on Election Day, the pro-Jesus Republican won 59 percent of the vote, defeating the anti-Jesus Democrat who earned 41 percent. Church voters swung the polls to a landslide election victory, and **voters fired eight legislators who had voted against a chaplains' right** to pray in Jesus' name.

While fund-raising we gathered fourteen thousand paper petitions for delivery to the new governor, who kept his pledge and restored six chaplain jobs, with freedom to pray in Jesus' name. We won. We liberated Virginia. So can you.

One thousand rallied for liberty and won with six police chaplains in Virginia

TOOL: CHOOSE YOUR ARENA
THE SEVEN MOUNTAINS OF INFLUENCE

You may be called to climb one of seven mountains.

"In 1975, Bill Bright, founder of Campus Crusade for Christ (now called Cru), and Loren Cunningham, founder of Youth with a Mission, had lunch together in Colorado. God simultaneously gave each of these change agents a message to give to the other. During that same time frame Francis Schaeffer was given a similar message: If we are to impact any nation for Jesus Christ, then we would have to affect the seven spheres, or mountains of society that are the pillars of any society."[3]

Every Christian is uniquely called by God to establish God's kingdom, but the place in society where your influence is most impactful is likely in one of seven categories:

1. Religion: You may be called by God to fill one of the five-fold gifts of Ephesians 4:11, as an apostle, prophet, evangelist, pastor, or

teacher. If you feel called in one of these areas, attend Bible college or surround yourself with Godly mentors that will help you preach the gospel of Jesus Christ and biblical truth without compromise. You establish Christ's kingdom by winning souls and building Christ's church, the people of God.

2. Government: You may be called by God to run for office or organize communities around certain issues or mobilize God's people to vote and establish God's law as our own, and God's kingdom on earth as it is in heaven. This book will help you.

3. Family: The highest noble calling of families is for men to love their wives, wives to respect their husbands, parents to train their children in the way they should go, and everyone to demonstrate Christ's love to the world by loving Christ together as a family.

4. Media: Don't complain about false reporters. Instead *become the media*. You don't need a journalism degree to start a blog or a podcast or even an online TV show. Grow your own e-mail list and report the good news to your own growing crowd.

5. Education: Teachers are the second greatest influence after parents. They can impact so many more hundreds or thousands of

students over a lifetime. Don't teach heresy or wrongdoing; teach Christ's commands.

6. Business: It's not just about making money so you can tithe to charity. Businesses also employ people, do good for the community and change lives through products, services, and mentoring good character. The more good you do, the more money God will entrust to your team. Grow your corporation for Christ!

7. Entertainment: There is so much evil in the arts; they recruit followers to sin. Wouldn't it be wonderful if godly artists inspired others to holiness and recruited followers to Christ?

Which of the above seven mountains will you devote your life to climb?

<u>Pray this prayer</u>: *"Father in heaven, show me your specific plan for my life, and call me to that ministry that makes the greatest impact for my own unique gifts and abilities. God help me choose my arena and climb one of the seven mountains. In Jesus' name, amen."*

<u>Assignment</u>: *Pray about which mountain to climb. Devote yourself to becoming an expert in your arena, and liberating it fully. Church arise! Let's liberate these seven mountains.*

<u>Get Credit</u>: *Write 25 to 40 words engaging with ideas in this chapter and e-mail them to* homework@ schoolofliberty.org *under the email subject "Liberate Chapter 7."*

If you engage with all 30 chapters, we'll make you a "Certified Liberty Instructor." You might earn pay. Visit http://SchoolOfLiberty.org to learn more.

WRITE YOUR PERSONAL NOTES AND QUESTIONS BELOW:

TOOL: BE AN ACTIVIST
THE FOUR: GOV'T, MEDIA, CITIZENS, ACTIVISTS

Four types of people engage in politics, but the last one, the activist, can be the most powerful.

1. **The Government:** Representatives are elected by earning popular votes to represent and make or amend laws that govern and rule the masses. You may think these people are omnipotent, but thankfully their power is limited by several factors: (a) They need consensus with other officials; (b) They need votes to be re-elected; (c) They need money to buy advertising to ensure re-election; and (d) They have healthy fear of losing the next election should they fail to represent people well. It is this healthy fear that keeps most incumbents in check. They are reined in by others who can help or hurt their political careers.

2. **The Media:** With the benefit of mass communication, the media can mislead many people so quickly that government officials have little time to react, and suddenly their political careers can be in danger. Honest media simply report the facts, but dishonest media seize power for themselves by getting their friends elected or enemies unelected. Only honest reporting breeds long-term public trust.

3. **The Citizens:** God bless them. Many citizens are often too busy earning a living and raising a family to care about politics. That is until some politician or policy makes them angry or concerned enough to rise up and fire their representative and hire a trustworthy replacement. Apathy can be overcome by information and good messaging that inspires patriotism.

4. **The Activist:** The activists can be the most powerful of the four types of people who engage in politics. The activist has an agenda, sometimes bad and sometimes good. Christian activists are called to establish the kingdom of Christ on earth, which is the highest good for all society. The Christian activist prays daily and looks for opportunities to take action, perhaps covertly at first but

eventually some issue they touch will land in the newspaper headlines. Their tools are protesting, assembling, petitioning, writing, speaking, interviewing, mobilizing, mass communicating, and occasionally doing a crazy act that grabs a headline. Rosa Parks' refusal to sit in the back of the bus gave her more power than the entire government of her day. Martin Luther King Jr. changed the world by volunteering for jail. Why? If one activist can get traction in the media, which angers or inspires the citizens who demand immediate action from government, the government will bow their knee to public pressure. Truth be told, one well-trained activist can become more powerful than the highest elected official.

<u>Pray this Prayer</u>: *"Father in heaven, I haven't fully considered the powerful potential of my own calling as an activist for your cause. Show me the depth of my own potential and give me the vision, passion, and strategy to become an effective political activist for You. In Jesus' name, amen."*

<u>Assignment</u>: *Pray and fast for three days about becoming a devoted, professional activist for your cause. Start small and say yes to God, then grow into that calling.*

<u>Get Credit:</u> *Write 25 to 40 words engaging with ideas in this chapter and e-mail them to* homework@schoolofliberty.org *under the email subject "Liberate Chapter 8."*

If you engage with all 30 chapters, we'll make you a "Certified Liberty Instructor." You might earn pay. Visit http://SchoolOfLiberty.org to learn more.

WRITE YOUR PERSONAL NOTES AND QUESTIONS BELOW:

VICTORY STORY

OVERRULING A MAYOR
IN CALIFORNIA

Many leftist atheist groups have noticed we outnumber them. There are far more Christians in America than unbelievers, so our candidates win elections and theirs don't. Atheists resort to filing lawsuits, often frivolous, against religious freedom. Sadly, sometimes they find a leftist judge who hates our constitutional freedom of religious expression and win in court. It's rare, but when a judge improperly rules that the Constitution strikes down religious freedom, we have two options: We can appeal the bad decision up to the Supreme Court, or we can petition legislators to write a better law.

Take for example, the case of the anti-Jesus Mayor Larry Hansen of Lodi, California. In the years following our victories for military chaplains, hospital chaplains, and police chaplains, atheist complainers began targeting regular citizen pastors, especially those who prayed "in Jesus' name" before city council meetings or state legislatures.

Atheist lawyers wrote angry letters to dozens of mayors across the whole state of California, threatening to sue each town unless each mayor banned the name of Jesus. Most mayors ignored the letters as the empty threats they were. But the cowardly mayor of Lodi banned local pastors who pray in Jesus' name from giving public invocations.

When I found out, I blew him up with press releases, exposing his cowardice and anti-Jesus discrimination, which really was illegal and unconstitutional, as the Supreme Court later ruled. But this mayor was stubborn and ignored bad press.

A Christian's strength is in God and numbers, not lawyerly procedure, so I did not threaten a lawsuit. Instead I mobilized a crowd. We fund-raised and rented Christian e-mail lists to gather a thousand petitions to each city councilor in Lodi, demanding they restore freedom for pastors to pray in Jesus' name. The anti-Jesus mayor ignored our petitions, so I organized local pastors to meet with the mayor privately to request he restore freedom. Because the mayor refused to listen to countless pastors from his own town, I flew to California and organized a rally on the steps of city hall. Over four hundred people attended, and city councilors remarked they'd never had overflow seating for a city council meeting such as that day. But the mayor and city council ignored their citizens.

Finally, I wrote each city council member personally, threatening to buy billboards along the highway during the next election, listing the names of any councilor or mayor who voted against the citizens' right to pray publicly in Jesus' name. The mayor finally repented, and the council voted 5-0 to restore freedom. The empty-threat atheist complainers never sued. Liberty won. This hardline billboard strategy God gave me to hold the councilors accountable to their voters reminded me of Ronald Reagan who once said, "If you can't make them see the light, make them feel the heat."

Four hundred citizens rallied for liberty and won at city council in Lodi, California

TOOL: GET INTERVIEWS
HOW TO WRITE A PRESS RELEASE

The media, particularly press reporters, crave a scoop. Their livelihood often depends on access to a celebrity or "the newsmaker" for a story in order to sell papers. A good activist always tells the truth, but also looks for controversy to jump into for the sake of their cause. Controversy sells papers, so it also attracts honest reporters. To get press you need to build relationships by being transparent, honest, and make a list of good reporters' phone numbers and e-mails you can contact whenever you become aware of (or you create) newsworthy events that help your cause.

Plan your news interviews. Make your sound bites short, punchy, and memorable. **Short:** don't drone on and on; they have limited print space. **Punchy:** use colorful words and analogies that make instant impact in the mind of the reader or listener. **Memorable:** the shock value of a good controversy should leave the reader feeling an emotional reaction. Do not "use" reporters but give them mutual benefit and value for their time. Offer but never demand or threaten. Let them say no but be willing to offer a twenty-four-hour exclusive if they promise to write your story first.

Ask the reporter to agree whether you are "on the record" (what you say can be quoted in print), "off the record" (they agree to not print what you say), or "on-background, not for attribution" (they can print your quote but not identify your name as a source). Good reporters will agree, if they want your quote.

A press release is not a complete story but a three-hundred-word summary designed to hook a reporter's interest so they call you for an interview. Write a short paragraph without the entire story but just a basic tease, who-what-when-where-why, and make it short, punchy, and memorable. Start by targeting print, with real papers and honest reporters. Leak it to just one reporter who writes for your target audience and give them an hour to respond. If they're busy or not interested, go to your second-best reporter. Again give them an hour to decline, but to give them an incentive, you might promise a twenty-four-hour exclusive before offering it to other papers. If it gets traction in print, radio or TV interviews may follow. If everyone declines, write an op–ed for your local paper. You can always blog for your own e-mail audience, but wouldn't you rather reach theirs first? Here are elements of a good press release:

Title/Subtitle (shocking headline grabs attention)
CITY, State, Date, (Newswire) –
Opening paragraph, who, what, when, where, why
Juicy quote from celebrity or activist
Web link to original documents proving facts
Standard description of your group (optional)
Contact information for booking interviews: Name, e-mail, phone number, website.
These three words: "For immediate release"

Pray this prayer: *"Father in heaven, give me good relationships with honest reporters who will tell Your side of the story and reach the multitudes. In Jesus' name, amen."*

Assignment: *Go to* http://ChristianNewsWire.com *to review samples. Copy their format.*

Get Credit: *Write 25 to 40 words engaging with ideas in this chapter and e-mail them to* homework@ schoolofliberty.org *under the email subject "Liberate Chapter 9."*

If you engage with all 30 chapters, we'll make you a "Certified Liberty Instructor." You might earn pay. Visit http://SchoolOfLiberty.org to learn more.

WRITE YOUR PERSONAL NOTES AND QUESTIONS BELOW:

DAY 10

TOOL: MAKE NEWS
YOU MUST BECOME THE MEDIA

I f a tree fell in the woods but nobody heard it, did it really fall? If a world-changing event happened around your cause but no reporter covered it, it never happened. You must get your events historicized in print or nobody will react and nothing will change. Your injustice will not be fixed.

There are many news outlets today, and each one has their niche. If you can get the attention of any *New York Times, Washington Post,* or *Washington Times* reporter (which is difficult), you may still get mixed results in print. They have big circulations, but the story won't always be favorable to your cause. Any local paper is a good start, and no press is worse than bad press. Certain news outlets, such as OneNewsNow, SRN News, WND.com, PIJN News, Fox News, are more favorable to Christians. You can also call your local talk radio hosts, or even national call-in shows (don't be shy), but ultimately if you want your story told your way, *you* must become the media.

Create your own blog online. You can do this for free through several different sites. There you can write and publish news alerts about your cause. It's important to do this daily to keep followers informed. The more you post the more you will grow your following. Stop informing your followers and your crowd dissipates. Content, content, content is king if you want readership. Set up an email subscription service so people can subscribe for updates. Collect e-mail addresses and e-blast your regular readers often, using MailChimp.com or ConstantContact.com (or some real political pros use PoliticalMedia.com to avoid getting shut down for too many spam complaints). Study monetization strategies, but only after you have a real crowd that reads your free content daily. Don't write to get rich; write to change the world and the followers will fund your cause, eventually.

Use every social media platform that gets results, starting with Facebook, Twitter, YouTube, and Instagram, but don't spend a lot of money to get clicks or views. Grow your followership organically over time. You do this by posting real content, content, content, and encourage readers to share your posts or Tweets with their friends. Content that shocks the senses is most likely to go viral; if it's dull and boring (or false) your readership will not return.

Grow your e-mail list. Start with friends and family, but expect them to be replaced by strangers who care more about your cause than your friends and family do. God will inspire select people to join your activist movement.

The conservative movement online is morphing daily but God's Word does not change, so if your new media group wants to make an eternal difference, stick with godly issues and biblical morality. Now go tell the world about Christ in today's culture. I started with a simple e-newsletter and today I host a national daily half-hour TV show on satellite TV. *You can too.*

Pray this prayer: *"Father in heaven, I want to communicate your vision about my cause to the world. Give me the strategy and methods to reach millions. In Jesus' name, amen."*

Assignment: *Open a free MailChimp or ConstantContact e-mail blasting account, and organize your email list to receive your great content on a regular basis in their inbox.*

Get Credit: *Write 25 to 40 words engaging with ideas in this chapter and e-mail them to* homework@ schoolofliberty.org *under the email subject "Liberate Chapter 10."*

If you engage with all 30 chapters, we'll make you a "Certified Liberty Instructor." You might earn pay. Visit http://SchoolOfLiberty.org to learn more.

WRITE YOUR PERSONAL NOTES AND QUESTIONS BELOW:

VICTORY STORY

OVERTURNING CITY COUNCIL
IN OKLAHOMA

The following is part of an op-ed I wrote for WND. com after the Tulsa city council banned "Jesus" prayers, (also fully available here: http://bit.ly/tulsajesus).

When a liberal chaplain who had controlled the rotating schedule for visiting pastors began enforcing the "no Jesus" prayer policy, it blew up in the Tulsa World newspaper. The Rev. Danny Lynchard admitted, "The phrase 'in Jesus' name' made it a non-inclusive prayer," so religious leaders who did not comply were removed from the rotation. Never one to shy from controversy, I sounded the alarm by granting my own newspaper interview and vowed to mobilize Tulsa-area pastors to stand up for Jesus and take back their government, even if I had to fly to Oklahoma myself.

At least one Tulsa pastor, Mark Rollins, took up my challenge and appeared personally before the

City Council to read the newspaper's exposure of anti-Jesus discrimination. "I'm upset about this," Rollins told the councilmembers, "you can't tell people to stop praying to Jesus. I know dozens of pastors in this town, and they won't stand for this."

Rollins then invited me to Tulsa and I stayed in his home. Together we prayed and watched the next council meeting on a local cable television network. Fireworks ensued. The City Council took 45 minutes to debate the issue, and opened the floor to 10 citizens, including eight liberals who came together, pleading to keep the 20-year-old ban in place.

The Oklahoma Conference for Community and Justice, or OCCJ, held a monopoly for decades, admitting they helped write the original policy that mandated 'non-sectarian' prayers. OCCJ Executive Director Nancy Day argued, "When asked to give a prayer in a public setting, you cannot assume everyone is of your faith. ... By praying to or through Jesus, that excludes folks in the room who are not Christian."

Apparently, she sees no irony in her own exclusion of praying Christians. But Councilor

John Eagleton countered with a brilliant legal defense of freedom, including case-law precedent, concluding, "I firmly believe that sanitized prayers to a generic deity don't really serve a spiritual purpose, at least not for me."

Public outcry from Christian citizens apparently won the day when the council voted 7-2 to restore liberty, writing a new policy that permits praying 'in Jesus' name,' a model policy that could be copied by other public bodies:

> "The prayer leader may use the specific name of their god within the prayer, so long as it is not used in a manner to proselytize or advance, or to disparage any faith or belief or the particular tenets or beliefs of individual faiths," the new policy reads.[4]

I find it interesting that even in the Bible-belt in conservative Tulsa, there exist anti-Jesus liberals who want the government to silence and censor the content of a pastor's prayer. They did not object to Jewish or Muslim prayers, only Christian prayers. But we fought back, we blew it up in the press, we mobilized a crowd, and we petitioned officials to do the right thing. And they did, not only because the city council agreed with us, but they feared the size of our crowd come next election.

There is a passage in the gospels where the Pharisees hated Jesus so much they wanted to kill him. But they did not. Why not? The Bible records: "They looked for a way to arrest him, but they were afraid of the crowd because the people held that he was a prophet" (Matt. 21:46).

In ancient Israel, just like in modern Tulsa, the liberals may hate you, but you will win political battles because they fear your crowd. In both cases, liberty won. Jesus won. Pastors and citizens showed up and out-numbered the anti-Jesus haters. You can too.

Mark Rollins-Founder
Christ For Humanity

Pastor Mark Rollins took a stand for liberty and won in Tulsa, Oklahoma

DAY 11

TOOL: COURAGE
CIVIL DISOBEDIENCE: OBEY GOD, NOT MEN

There is a time and place for nonviolent civil disobedience to unjust laws. It's how bad laws get repealed. When activists say no to dictatorial government and break their phony "rules," it exposes tyrannical corruption. Newspapers cover the story, citizens get outraged and join your protest, and government caves in and changes the law. You can win, but **count the cost.** If you are a single parent with four children, you can't go to jail often. If you can't afford to get fired from your job, don't intentionally anger your boss. Be wise as serpents, innocent as doves, and fear not. When God's Spirit wells up inside of you with righteous anger, turn over some tables in the public square. Jesus did. Sure, he got crucified, but he also received resurrection power.

Obey civil authorities and police and laws that agree with God and the Bible. The apostle Paul wrote,

Let everyone be subject to the governing authorities, for there is no authority except that which God has established. The authorities that exist have been established by God. Consequently, whoever rebels against the authority is rebelling against what God has instituted, and those who do so will bring judgment on themselves. For rulers hold no terror for those who do right, but for those who do wrong. Do you want to be free from fear of the one in authority? Then do what is right and you will be commended. For the one in authority is God's servant for your good. But if you do wrong, be afraid, for rulers do not bear the sword for no reason. They are God's servants, agents of wrath to bring punishment on the wrongdoer. Therefore, it is necessary to submit to the authorities, not only because of possible punishment but also as a matter of conscience. (Romans 13:1–5)

In other words, get punished for doing right and preaching Christ, but not for robbing a liquor store. Disobey unjust authorities that insist you disobey God. Follow Peter and John's example in Acts 4-5:

Then they called them in again and commanded them not to speak or teach at all in the name of Jesus. But Peter and John replied, "Which is right in God's eyes: to listen to you, or to him? You be the judges! As for us, we cannot help speaking about what we have seen and heard. (Acts 4:18–20)

Peter and John were ordered to stop preaching Christ, but they disobeyed men and obeyed God.

Peter and the other apostles replied: "We must obey God rather than human beings!" . . . They called the apostles in and had them flogged. Then they ordered them not to speak in the name of Jesus, and let them go. The apostles left the Sanhedrin, rejoicing because they had been counted worthy of suffering disgrace for the Name. (Acts 5:29, 40–41)

Notice they rejoiced in suffering for doing right, but they didn't get violent toward their persecutors. They peacefully kept preaching Christ. They took their beating, and were eventually martyred, but today their example is still liberating the world. They were activists following their chief Activist who was also criminalized for doing right. Are you His disciple?

Pray this prayer: "*Father in heaven, give me fearless courage to obey God always, even if I must disobey human authority on rare occasion. Give me wisdom to avoid needless persecution, but when the time comes, help me stand tall. In Jesus' name, amen.*"

Assignment: *Name and study three modern Christian activists who have suffered.*

<u>Get Credit</u>: *Write 25 to 40 words engaging with ideas in this chapter and e-mail them to* homework@ schoolofliberty.org *under the email subject "Liberate Chapter 11."*

If you engage with all 30 chapters, we'll make you a "Certified Liberty Instructor." You might earn pay. Visit http://SchoolOfLiberty.org to learn more.

WRITE YOUR PERSONAL NOTES AND QUESTIONS BELOW:

TOOL: FEDERALISM
THE DOCTRINE OF THE LESSER
MAGISTRATE

C ivil disobedience is generally when citizens disobey unjust human authority in order to obey God. The Doctrine of the Lesser Magistrate is when locally elected or appointed city, county, or state officials interpret existing human laws differently than higher level officials, and they exercise the power of their lower office to contradict higher opinions. Federalism authorizes lower governments to disagree with higher authorities, and fight Constitutional differences in court. There are political risks for stands taken by brave lower officials, but often local authorities can appeal and win in courts, beating back the higher authorities overreach or faulty interpretation of true law. If you are a local official, we hereby call upon you to promote true justice regardless of personal risk.

According to historian-theologian Matt Trewhella:

The Lesser Magistrate Doctrine teaches that when the superior or higher ranking civil authority makes immoral/unjust laws or policies, the lower or lesser ranking civil authority has both a right and duty to refuse obedience to that superior authority. If necessary, the lesser authorities may even actively resist the higher authority.

God has established four realms of government to which He delegates authority. They are: (1) self-government; (2) family government; (3) church government; and (4) civil government. Each has its own role, function, and jurisdiction. The authority an individual possesses in any one of these four realms of government is delegated authority. In other words, they derive their authority from God. Their authority is not autonomous or unconditional. Their authority is God-given, and thus, they have a duty to govern in accordance with His rule. When someone in authority makes laws or decrees contrary to God's law, they are in rebellion to God's rule. Those under their authority are NOT to obey them when they do this. They may have to even actively resist them.[5]

Modern examples of this doctrine abound.

Alabama Supreme Court Justice Roy Moore refused to remove God's Ten Commandments from a public display, defying federal judges who ordered that removal in violation of the Tenth Amendment. Judge Moore was removed from office but later vindicated by the people of Alabama who elected him again and restored him to the same office.

Kentucky Clerk Kim Davis refused to personally sign homosexual marriage certificates and endured five days in jail for disobeying a higher judge's order that she must violate her conscience. Clerk Davis was later vindicated when state laws were changed, restoring freedom of conscience and allowing state employees to opt out of participation.

Navy Chaplain Gordon "Chaps" Klingenschmitt prayed publicly "in Jesus' name" in uniform, violating a bad Navy prayer policy that prohibited "worshipping in public" and banned "sectarian" prayers that mention the name of Jesus outside of Sunday chapel. After enduring misdemeanor court-martial and losing his career and pension, Chaps was vindicated by Congress who rescinded the Navy's prayer policy and restored freedom of speech for other chaplains.

> Pray this prayer: *"Father in heaven, I pray for those brave local officials willing to defend the Constitution at great personal risk. Give them victory. In Jesus' name, amen."*

> Assignment: *Research other historical examples at* http://lessermagistrate.com.

> Get Credit: *Write 25 to 40 words engaging with ideas in this chapter and e-mail them to* homework@ schoolofliberty.org *under the email subject "Liberate Chapter 12."*

If you engage with all 30 chapters, we'll make you a "Certified Liberty Instructor." You might earn pay. Visit http://SchoolOfLiberty.org to learn more.

WRITE YOUR PERSONAL NOTES AND QUESTIONS BELOW:

VICTORY STORY

PA PASTOR DEFIES SPEAKER
OF THE HOUSE

One day the Pennsylvania Speaker of the House of Pennsylvania Democrat Keith McCall invited a local pastor, Gerry Stoltzfoos, to come and pray the invocation before the opening gavel. The pastor agreed and was asked to submit a written copy of his proposed prayer beforehand for "screening" to make sure it didn't offend anybody. When the Speaker read that the pastor's prayer would end "in Jesus' name," the anti-Jesus McCall disinvited the pastor and canceled the prayer.

But Pastor Stoltzfoos was not intimidated. He told the newspapers and blew the whistle on the anti-Jesus speaker's illegal and unconstitutional censorship. I read the headlines: "State House edits 'Jesus' from pastor's prayer"[6] and "Pa. House prayer rejected over 'Jesus.'"[7] Having been in his shoes before, I knew what to do. I took action.

I did not fly to Pennsylvania, but I bought the email lists of many conservatives who lived in Pennsylvania, and I sent them a simple alert. I asked one hundred thousand voters to sign a free online petition we had created. We got about one thousand signatures. I put the name and address of each petition signee at the bottom of their petition, one citizen per page, and printed off all one thousand pages. I then obtained the direct fax numbers of all 203 members of the Pennsylvania state house, and all 50 state senators. We then proceeded to fax all one thousand petitions to each of the 253 members, delivering 253,000 pieces of paper directly to their desks within a week's time.

I helped Pennsylvania citizens communicate directly with their own elected officials, and using their own paper buried them in petitions. The pro-Jesus Christians of Pennsylvania rose up and stood with the brave pastor, demanding religious freedom of speech and the right to pray "in Jesus' name." Then something wonderful happened.

I am told that Speaker Keith McCall, a Democrat, held private meetings with his own members, who pressured him to reverse his anti-Jesus ban, which had caused public outrage and endangered many representatives' re-election campaigns. McCall decided he could not personally stand for reelection and quit the house after just two years as speaker.

The Speaker also reversed his policy. He contacted Pastor Stoltzfoos and not only apologized but personally invited the pastor to come back to the state house and pray publicly "in Jesus' name." We won. Liberty was restored. But the brave pastor respectfully declined Speaker McCall's offer to say the prayer in the state house. Instead he accepted another offer and prayed in the state senate. And he prayed "in Jesus' name." Victories like this happen only when Christians stand up to their elected officials together. Jesus wins. You can too.

Pastor Gerry Stoltzfoos took a stand for liberty and won in Pennsylvania

DAY 13

TOOL: INCORPORATE
CREATE AN ORGANIZATION

Organizations may be informal groups of people, but formally incorporated groups often have extra levels of legal protection that allow them decreased liability and increased credibility in the eyes of donors. Corporations are easy to create. You just file notarized copies of your articles of incorporation with your secretary of state, and abide by self-imposed bylaws that direct your board and officers.

Churches do not need to incorporate to receive tax exemptions in America, but most do, so they can pay their employees and file appropriate payroll taxes, and donors can document and claim a tax deduction on their annual income taxes. Churches are less limited than 501c(3) organizations and generally should not try to become 501c(3)s.

Nonprofit charities (other than churches) are often incorporated under section 501c(3) of the IRS code. These are often religious or educational in mission and avoid direct political activism, which they are prohibited from doing at an expense of over 5 percent of its annual budget. They can instantly receive tax-deductible donations, but it takes five years to attain permanent recognition status with the IRS. They get fantastic bulk-rate postage discounts, and donors can claim tax deductions. They must document every penny on public annual IRS reports.

Not-for-profit "social welfare" educational charities incorporated under section 501c(4) of the IRS code often speak a more political issue message but are still prohibited from directly endorsing or campaigning for candidates for public office with more than 5 percent of their annual budget. Their donors do not receive tax-deductible exemptions, but these corporations do not pay taxes like for-profit corporations would.

Political Action Committees (PACs) or Small Donor Committees are corporations that can raise limited non-tax-deductible donations (perhaps $50 or $400 per donor per year, depending on your state laws) and spend limited amounts helping candidates get elected (perhaps $2500 per year per candidate). They are usually organized around a specific political issue, so they donate to several candidates who share their values and would likely legislate for that issue if elected.

Independent Expenditure Committees (IECs) are corporations usually organized under US Tax Code 527 that can receive unlimited, large, non-deductible donations. They are usually formed by very wealthy people who want to publish widely a message about a candidate but may not coordinate with candidates.

Candidate campaign committees are formed by candidates running for office and may receive limited non-tax-deductible donations that vary by state.

Pray this prayer: *"Father in heaven, I want to learn the rules and properly pay taxes as Jesus said, 'render to Caesar what is Caesar's and to God what is God's.' Help me understand how to incorporate the right kind of organization to fulfill my group's particular mission, for maximum efficiency and impact. In Jesus' name, amen."*

Assignment: *Visit* http://nolo.com *or* http://legalzoom.com *and incorporate a group.*

Get Credit: *Write 25 to 40 words engaging with ideas in this chapter and e-mail them to* homework@schoolofliberty.org *under the email subject "Liberate Chapter 13."*

If you engage with all 30 chapters, we'll make you a "Certified Liberty Instructor." You might earn pay. Visit http://SchoolOfLiberty.org to learn more.

WRITE YOUR PERSONAL NOTES AND QUESTIONS BELOW:

TOOL: WEBSITE
CREATE A WEBSITE TO GET THE WORD OUT

I f you're not online, people can't find you, even if they want to, with rare exception. If you are online, everybody can find you, and they may want to help. To create a popular movement, go where people are.

It's so easy to create a website these days, nearly every American has one or several. Even if you don't host your own website, you can start journaling on a weblog (blog) hosted on other publishers' sites. Just google "blog hosting," and soon you'll be publishing your opinions for the world to read. Nearly everyone has Facebook or Twitter accounts, but vain people spend more time "tweeting" than reading other people's tweets. Facebook can be a great time-waster if you spend hours daily arguing with the same ten friends, even if you think you have thousands of followers.

Good activists are producers, not just consumers. The purpose of your website is to publish great unique content and to receive donations that grow your ability to push out that content to a wider audience. If you can't do that well, hire someone who can or support others who can and join their team. But if you have a gift for writing unique messages that inspire and if you feel God is calling you, then create your own website and change the world for Christ.

First, reserve a short but memorable domain name (website address or URL, such as SchoolOfLiberty.org or PrayInJesusName.org) at any site registrar like Register.com, GoDaddy.com, or NetworkSolutions.com. End your site name with .com if you're for-profit or .org if you're nonprofit. (I would avoid less popular domain endings like .net, .biz, or .us, simply because they don't seem to rank as high on search engines.)

Once your name is reserved, you need to hire a host that will store your data and display it from their servers to the eyeballs of your customers. Bluehost.com, Web.com, GoDaddy.com, or EHost.com seem to be popular, but google "host a website" for more options. Once you choose a host, you need an expert who builds websites that you can edit it later. Ask your friends for local recommendations, but the best guy is not always the cheapest. If someone says, "I can build you a website for one thousand dollars," they may or may not deliver, so get recommendations from other customers. Ask them if they build in "Wordpress," which is user-friendly, or "Wix.com," which is also easy to edit later, or simply "HTML," which could be hard for you to learn if you're new at this.

Create a Paypal.com account linked to your nonprofit bank account, and post their donate button on your site. Or use Piryx or Anedot or other credit-card processing system for your donate button, and make it BIG on your site. Also post your cause at any or all ten sites mentioned at http://crowdfunding.com.

If you're stuck, ask a young person you trust, because millennials grew up with HTML. They can code in their sleep; they "get it," or their friends do.

Pray this prayer: *"Father in heaven, I may not be a web-site expert, but somebody I know is. I ask you to connect me with the right designer. In Jesus' name, amen."*

Assignment: *Ask three web-savvy friends for a referral to their favorite site-designer.*

Get Credit: *Write 25 to 40 words engaging with ideas in this chapter and e-mail them to* homework@ schoolofliberty.org *under the email subject "Liberate Chapter 14."*

If you engage with all 30 chapters, we'll make you a "Certified Liberty Instructor." You might earn pay. Visit http://SchoolOfLiberty.org to learn more.

WRITE YOUR PERSONAL NOTES AND QUESTIONS BELOW:

VICTORY STORY

CHURCHES RALLY FOR FREEDOM
IN OREGON

One day after a pastor prayed "in Jesus name" before the meeting of the city council of Baker City, Oregon, the council received a complaint from an easily offended anti-Jesus complainer. The city was afraid of a lawsuit, so they temporarily banned some prayer-givers who they feared might speak that "illegal" word, the name of Jesus, at future meetings. They even created a policy requiring "non-sectarian" prayers only, so the government censored prayer speech and required only prayers to a neutered god.

When I read about the anti-Jesus speech ban, I leapt into action. I did not fly to Oregon but simply dialed the phone numbers of every evangelical pastor I could find in that city. One pastor, Roger Scovil, not only took my call but vowed on the phone he would mobilize a crowd. Many other pastors joined him. And after I alerted the great OneNewsNow reporter Charlie Butts, they published this victory report:

"Prayers will continue at the Baker City, Oregon, Council meetings despite an attempt to have the issue put to the voters.

"According to the *Baker City Herald*, Baker City resident Gary Dielman was offended by a council meeting prayer that ended with "in Jesus' name, amen." . . . However, councilors ultimately decided to keep the opening prayer, and, after reviewing the council's "Invocation Guidelines," they decided to remove the word "non-sectarian." Council members also decided not to send the issue to the voters.

"The issue drew a large crowd to the Council meeting and an outpouring of public support for the opening prayer. Pastor Roger Scovil of Baker City Christian Church applauds the Council's decision. 'I've seen many rulings in communities across the country where praying in Jesus' name is being disallowed out of interest in being all inclusive and not offending or excluding anyone,' he notes.

"Scovil and two other pastors spoke before the Council and a packed chamber. "[A]nd [the speech was] well received by the City Council, even those who are not necessarily identified as Christians.

"The *Herald* quoted Scovil as saying, during the Council meeting, "In the name of freedom, allow people to pray according to the teachings of their faith and their conscience.

"The pastor says he finds it hard to believe that organizations such as the American Civil Liberties Union are so successful in frightening government bodies into secular prayers, or none at all." [8]

This example from real events shows the importance of asking pastors to get involved in their local community meetings, especially when atheist complainers demand we be censored or silenced. When religious freedom is attacked, pastors must rise up!

Pastor Scovil showed great courage, mobilized a crowd, even the nonbelieving officials took note and feared offending angry church voters, and city council voted 5-0 to strike "non-sectarian" and allow Jesus prayers.

Free speech won. Liberty won. Jesus won. And the anti-Jesus complainer never sued. The toothless paper tigers rarely do. Our crowds, our faith, and our God are greater, if we only rise to occupy the land. Will you ask your pastor to get involved in politics, or at least allow his church to defend religious freedom?

Pastor Roger Scovil took a stand for liberty and won in Baker City, Oregon

TOOL: E-MAIL LIST
BUILD AN ARMY WITH AN E-MAIL LIST

A leader without followers is just taking a walk.

If you don't have troops backing your cause, nobody will listen. If they do listen, it's for pity not respect. If you want to earn political respect, you must lead a crowd.

The other day my friend called her congressman and said, "I have five thousand followers for my cause on Facebook." Do you think she got a meeting? Yes! Traction is measured in numbers of readers, signers, donors, and when your cause goes viral, the powerful elites may begin calling you, you won't always have to call them.

Remember from Day 10 that forwarded emails can help get major traction. People still read e-mails; everybody's got an inbox. They check it every few hours. They have at least ten e-mail buddies they forward to, friends ready to click on *your* link to your site where they can sign your petition or donate. If you did your Day 10 assignment, you now have a MailChimp or ConstantContact e-mail blasting account, and you've sent out a few test e-mails to your best list of friends' e-mails. Now take it to the next level.

Once you have a fully functioning website or at least a bare-bones "landing page," where you want people to click, read, and take action, you are ready to create a juicy, brief, inspiring e-mail messages that can be read by dozens (or thousands) of friends for your cause. *Don't* spam people with useless jokes or garbage to make them unsubscribe (or worse, to make them click spam which reports you to the internet cops who will shut you down). Rather begin to create daily useful content people will want, so rather than unsubscribing, they will cherish your alerts.

Daily? Weekly? Monthly? I e-mail twenty-five thousand people daily, and they don't unsubscribe because it's useful and newsy. Yet most people only open 10 to 15 percent of all e-mails they receive, so make sure your subject line really sings. Remember "short, punchy, memorable" and you'll increase your open rates to 20 percent, and earn more forwarded e-mails by friends telling friends.

Content drives readership, period. Your content should be "red meat" for your target audience, so juicy they cannot help but return for tomorrow's update. If it gets their blood boiling, they'll click or donate. That's not always the goal, but it might be. Remember people rally to a cause, *their* cause, not necessarily to a leader's personality. I'm not a handsome movie star. I'm balding with a potbelly, but I lead a growing crowd because I can write daily content that gets people fired up. I look for stories that cause them to take action immediately because the outrage cannot be ignored; it must be defeated. I have an army. Power-brokers return my calls and take my meetings, and VIPs call me to get favorable coverage on my media show. We move the votes in DC and in homes across America. That's leadership. Others with no army are just pretenders.

> Pray this prayer: *"Father in heaven, I want to lead large crowds of people, which requires communicating with them effectively and regularly. Give me inspiring words and an efficient platform to write or speak to your people daily. In Jesus' name, amen."*

> Assignment: *Commit to daily e-mail blasting. Practice daily e-mail blasting.*

> Get Credit: *Write 25 to 40 words engaging with ideas in this chapter and e-mail them to* homework@ schoolofliberty.org *under the email subject "Liberate Chapter 15."*

> *If you engage with all 30 chapters, we'll make you a "Certified Liberty Instructor." You might earn pay. Visit http://SchoolOfLiberty.org to learn more.*

WRITE YOUR PERSONAL NOTES AND QUESTIONS BELOW:

DAY 16

TOOL: PETITIONS
PETITIONS GROW YOUR BASE

One secret to building your army is to recruit, motivate, and activate online petition signers. A simple online petition can (a) sort the wheat from the chaff by helping you find like-minded citizens for your cause; (b) allow you to collect new names, e-mails, and phone numbers of new friends to grow your list; and (c) give you clout before members of Congress or elected officials who respect your audience full of voters.

Let's imagine two phone calls to a congressman. One is from a citizen who stands alone. The other is from a citizen with a list of one thousand people who signed his petition for his cause. Which phone call gets returned faster? Delivering a health stack of petitions gives you and your cause instant credibility, and moves you to the front of the line to get things done. You'll get a meeting, rather than getting ignored. Multiple citizens on your team can give you access to multiple congressmen, who can build a coalition and move a bill through committee. Thousands of citizens can actually join together to win elections or get a congressman fired if he opposes too many voters in his own district.

Politics is a numbers game, and if you're just starting out then petitions are a great tool to grow. Here are two kinds: (1) Informal petitions that are generally worded with a request for policymakers to take action for your cause, and (2) legal petitions that your state's secretary of state or local government's county clerk must pre-format, and petitioners must get notarized to get candidates or issues on a ballot for a vote. Ask your local officials about rules and procedures to change a law. They should want to help you.

Here are five ways to deliver an informal petition:

1. **E-mail** is instant and can generate numbers but is often blocked by filters.
2. **Phone calls** are blocked by secretaries or interns or become just a check mark on a tally sheet.
3. **Letters** end up in a stack of mail and take weeks to arrive if they even get past security screenings.
4. **Faxes** are quite effective, instant, and like letters actually are delivered on real paper like postal mail but may bypass the security blocker.
5. **Personal meetings** with your elected official, face to face over coffee or in a public meeting like a town hall are best.

I recommend faxes and personal meetings as most effective. But if you can't get a meeting, or don't have a fax machine, try using http://FaxCongress.com to create your own free e-petition. It converts your petition to a real fax delivered on their office paper instantly to your congressman's office. It also has a social dashboard to make your issue go viral among like-minded friends.

Pray this prayer: *"Father in heaven, you love our petitions, and I ask your help to make me an organizer of many, many people to petition for liberty. In Jesus' name, amen."*

Assignment: *Sign an online petition and create a free user account at* http://FaxCongress.com. *Then create your own petition and invite your friends to co-sign your FaxCongress petition to their congressman.*

Get Credit: *Write 25 to 40 words engaging with ideas in this chapter and e-mail them to* homework@ schoolofliberty.org *under the email subject "Liberate Chapter 16."*

If you engage with all 30 chapters, we'll make you a "Certified Liberty Instructor." You might earn pay. Visit http://SchoolOfLiberty.org to learn more.

WRITE YOUR PERSONAL NOTES AND QUESTIONS BELOW:

VICTORY STORY

OHIO SPEAKER REVERSED
BY JESUS' CROWD

On day a local pastor Rev. Keith Hamblen led an opening prayer before the Ohio state house and concluded his prayer, "in Jesus' name." His prayer was normal, but what caused a stir was when the anti-Jesus chairman of the state Democratic Party, Chris Redfern, walked off the floor in protest against Jesus and against religious freedom of speech. The next day, with or without permission from the Republican Speaker of the House, Jon Husted, the Ohio clerk of the House issued new prayer guidelines requiring "non-sectarian" prayer content, and a seventy-two-hour pre-screening and authorization period for each prayer offered.

"Prayers before the House should be nondenominational, nonsectarian, and nonproselytizing," the new Ohio guidelines said.[9] These guidelines established a 'heckler's veto' over the visiting pastor, giving unconstitutional power to any easily offended complainer who became the sole arbiter over whether his own ears were offended by the prayer. Students of the First Amendment will recognize that giving legal power to every random heckler in the crowd will silence the freedom of the speaker, and soon nobody will be allowed to speak for fear of offending the bully. So I took action.

I flew to Ohio and gave seventeen speeches to seventeen churches or religious groups in fourteen days, following instructions from Samuel Adams, a Founding Father who once said: "It does not take a majority to prevail, but rather an irate, tireless minority, keen on setting brushfires of freedom in the minds of men."

I wrote op-eds (for example this one at WND: http://bit.ly/ohiojesus) and gave out the phone numbers of the Republican Speaker Jon Husted, asking "will anybody in Ohio call his or her legislator at 1-800-282-0253, or contact them at house.state.oh.us?" My dear friend Chris Long at Ohio Christian Alliance also made calls, and it's good to know a respected lobbyist who can open doors of influence when you need it.

The ground game worked. I never met Speaker Husted, but I'm thankful that when he reconvened the Ohio State House in the fall of 2007, his first act of business was to reverse his own clerk's bad guidance and restore freedom to pray "in Jesus' name." He invited a pastor to pray without restriction, and that model policy has been in place ever since.

All credit belongs to Jesus Christ, in whose name we pray, because God the Father answered our prayers that religious liberty would be restored. God has commanded us to pray in faith expecting victory, and yet it's also wise to work, work, work for election victory, and hold accountable those in office to do right or face election defeat. Yes, I pray for a garden, but I also take a hoe to the ground, plant seeds, and water soil. In Ohio we restored liberty. *So can you.*

Rev. Keith Hamblen dared to pray "in Jesus' name" and was vindicated in Ohio

TOOL: EVENTS
ORGANIZE A RALLY

Have you seen on TV occasional crowds of people with metaphorical pitchforks and torches (or signs and banners) marching in the streets trying to get public attention for their cause? Such rallies don't just happen spontaneously. Leaders organize those events for weeks beforehand. Now picture yourself as that leader, organizing a peaceful rally.

It's not that hard to organize a rally, but it does take publicity to draw a crowd for your cause. Follow these simple steps:

1. Target one policy or policymaker to affect.
2. Decide your time, place, and audience.
3. Obtain any necessary permits; portable toilets; police, fire, medical supervision, if necessary.
4. Create a message, flyer, online ad strategy.
5. Market and promote your event like crazy.
6. Invite the press, cameras, reporters to come.

7.   Obey legal authorities and train non-violence.
8.   Collect names/emails of attendees for future events.

Two things might happen: (1) Your event is not well attended for lack of interest or marketing, or (2) your event is well attended, gets public attention for your cause, and leaders show up and change laws.

It's rare that officials will ignore a well-attended rally. It's more likely if elected officials see an angry but well-behaved crowd, they'll try to get in front to lead your parade. Let them. Give them a microphone, and encourage voters to donate to their re-election campaigns, but only if they help your cause. You want those leaders re-elected since they may fight for your cause inside the halls of power. If leaders hate your cause or crowd, vote them out and organize campaign activities to fire the obstacle politicians at the next election cycle.

The most important rally is the election. If your people don't show up and vote, or foolishly boycott the election, your cause will be harmed by political adversaries who pass opposing laws to ban your business, restrict your freedoms, and impose tyranny. Christians are called to liberate, which means voting for officials who will rescind bad restrictive laws, cut taxes, shrink the size of government, restore power to the people, and pass laws that help, not hurt our pro-liberty causes.

If you cannot organize real voters to win elections, you will not be feared, respected, or loved by officials. You will be ignored, or worse, ruled by tyrants. But if you can mobilize a crowd, especially on Election Day, God's people can govern the governors, keep the Republic, and liberate the oppressed by empowering them to hold their officials accountable.

Pray this prayer: *"Father in heaven, help me organize a peaceful crowd to show up at my event so that it makes an effective political statement. Give us favor with officials who will help fight for our cause, and help us change bad laws. In Jesus' name, amen."*

Assignment: *Hold a planning meeting with local activists to organize a rally event.*

Get Credit: *Write 25 to 40 words engaging with ideas in this chapter and e-mail them to* homework@schoolofliberty.org *under the email subject "Liberate Chapter 17."*

If you engage with all 30 chapters, we'll make you a "Certified Liberty Instructor." You might earn pay. Visit http://SchoolOfLiberty.org to learn more.

WRITE YOUR PERSONAL NOTES AND QUESTIONS BELOW:

TOOL: REPEATED ACTIONS
MOBILIZE YOUR ARMY TO DAILY ACTION

O ccasional events are powerful, but daily action is necessary to keep your crowd engaged. Too often a Christian attends an event but afterward goes home and falsely imagines the work is done. To preserve liberty you must elect more liberators and fire more tyrants. This requires daily work. It is your life's calling from God to liberate the oppressed. To make daily change happen, you must mobilize your "army." Here are some daily activist activities for leaders to mobilize your crowd:

1. E-mail your crowd with issue updates.
2. Create or modify new petitions.
3. Recruit new signers, attendees, volunteers.
4. Call, e-mail, or fax elected officials.
5. Schedule personal meetings with officials.
6. Draft proposed legislation for officials.
7. Meet and call officials' staff to follow up.

8. Visit the capitol weekly during legislative session.
9. Volunteer as intern staff working at the capitol.
10. Host recurring public meetings each month.
11. Invite officials to come talk to your crowd.
12. Testify at committee meetings as expert witness for or against legislation.
13. Track voting records of all elected officials.
14. Publish voting records at election season.
15. Visit your party headquarters to volunteer.
16. Volunteer on a campaign to help a candidate.
17. Work creatively against an obstacle candidate.
18. Knock on doors, make phone calls, donate money to elect champions.

It's wasteful to rally an army only to dissolve your crowd before the election. It's worse to dissolve your crowd after the election, especially if your candidate wins. Your "champion" elected officials likely remain outnumbered in the legislature and need help to govern, build coalitions, and lobby other officials during the legislative cycle. Keeping your crowd engaged to show up and do real political work can earn you clout and credible citizen power. "When the righteous thrive, people rejoice; when the wicked rule, the people groan" (Proverbs 29:2). Or as Jesus said (quoting Isaiah):

"The Spirit of the Lord is upon Me, Because He has anointed Me

To preach the gospel to the poor; He has sent Me to heal the brokenhearted,

To proclaim liberty to the captives, And recovery of sight to the blind,

To set at liberty those who are oppressed;

To proclaim the acceptable year of the LORD." (Luke 4:18–19, NKJV)

This was Christ's daily mission. Now it's yours.

<u>Pray this prayer</u>: *"Father in heaven, help me motivate and re-energize my followers to daily action that makes a real difference for liberty. In Jesus' name, amen."*

<u>Assignment</u>: *Research the legislative calendar to learn when your issues appear as good or bad legislation before committees at your state capitol. Ask to testify.*

<u>Get Credit</u>: *Write 25 to 40 words engaging with ideas in this chapter and e-mail them to* homework@ schoolofliberty.org *under the email subject "Liberate Chapter 18."*

If you engage with all 30 chapters, we'll make you a "Certified Liberty Instructor." You might earn pay. Visit http://SchoolOfLiberty.org to learn more.

WRITE YOUR PERSONAL NOTES AND QUESTIONS BELOW:

VICTORY STORY

NORTH CAROLINA PASTOR FIRED, RESTORED

In July 2010, just months before a mid-term election, the evangelical volunteer "chaplain for a week" at the North Carolina state legislature was fired by the Democrat Speaker after his first Monday on the job. The chaplain's crime? Praying "in Jesus' name" when invited to pray before the legislature. Fox News' Todd Starnes reported the story: "Pastor Yanked from Capitol over 'Jesus' Prayer'."[10]

Speaker Joe Hackney, a Democrat of thirty-two years in the legislature, instructed his clerk to tell Pastor Ron Baity, the chaplain, "your services will no longer be needed this week," and he was not allowed to finish his assigned week. Baity tells that story of who, when, and why he got fired in his own words, on video. (Watch: http://bit.ly/pastorbaity) At a press conference he cited several Scriptures: John 14:13–14, 15:16, and 16:23–26 in which Jesus instructs us to pray to the Father in Jesus' name. Baity told a crowd:

Whether it be in this church body . . . or whether it be in the legislature or the Capitol building we believe that prayer that is effective prayer on behalf of an individual or a nation must be offered in the name of Jesus Christ.[11]

Since I knew Pastor Ron Baity and had spoken in his church, I believed his story and took action. I did not fly to North Carolina, but just like our battles in Virginia and Pennsylvania, I gathered online petitions from local citizens and began burning up the fax lines to all 120 state representatives and fifty state senators. We buried so many legislators in fax paper listing the names of Christians who stood with Pastor Baity, demanding freedom to pray "in Jesus' name" that *my* phone began ringing off the hook from legislators who directly called me to say "enough, we get it."

But I didn't stop there. We faxed 3,082 pastors free North Carolina voter guides just before the election. And hundreds of pastors stood in their Sunday pulpit and encouraged Christians to vote, many naming the anti-Jesus Speaker of the House, Democrat Joe Hackney, as the obstacle to religious liberty.

In the November 2010 election, the North Carolina state house switched parties, proof here:

North Carolina House of Representatives		
Party	As of November 1, 2010	After the 2010 Election
Democratic Party	68	52
Republican Party	52	67
Independent	-	1
Total	120	120

Democrats have not held a majority in North Carolina since. Speaker Hackney retired. On opening day in January, the new Republican Speaker invited a former official to pray, "in Jesus' name." Pastor Ron Baity won, not only by restoring freedom to pray, but by mobilizing fellow pastors to take back the entire legislature. *So can you.*

Pastor Ron Baity took a stand for liberty and won
in North Carolina

DAY 19

TOOL: RULINGS
SUE FOR JUSTICE IN COURT

Thank God for Christian lawyers, the tip of the spear in American legal defense, who defend our constitutional rights and sue to overturn bad state or federal laws.

Oppressed Christians should sue nonbelieving tyrants in court to demand justice.

Let me say again.

Oppressed Christians should sue nonbelieving tyrants in court to demand justice.

While suing may seem shocking or unchristian, it's quite Christian to appeal to Caesar for justice. The Apostle Paul did it, and so did Jesus. I have never sued a Christian, but I routinely sue nonbelievers to try to obtain justice because I follow the example of the Apostle Paul, who wrote:

> If . . . I am guilty of doing anything deserving death, I do not refuse to die. But if the charges brought against me . . . are not true, no one has the right to hand me over to them. I appeal to Caesar!" (Acts 25:11)

Notice how Paul sued the unbelievers in court to defend his own right to preach the gospel. The exception is, don't sue other Christians if they accept mediation through any Church elders. (Read 1 Corinthians 6.)

Jesus told the parable of the persistent widow, who won favor with an ungodly judge, who said, "Even though I don't fear God or care what people think, yet because this widow keeps bothering me, I will see that she gets justice, so that she won't eventually come and attack me!" (Luke 18:4-5). Even ungodly judges may give you justice!

One of four things may happen in court:

1. You may win if a good judge enforces a good law.
2. You may lose if a bad judge enforces a bad law.
3. You may win if a good judge overturns bad law.
4. You may lose if a bad judge overturns good law.

My point here is that not all laws are godly, but some are. Neither are all judges godly, but some are. They key is to hire a good Christian lawyer and make the effort to win because if you win, you can reaffirm good law or strike down bad law, which has the effect of setting precedent to liberate other Christians in your situation in the future.

If the tyrannical oppressor loses in court, maybe they'll stop oppressing others in the future. If Christian florists and photographers and bakers cave in to tyranny and do not resist immoral punishment and do not fight back in court, their constitutional right to religious freedom will be trampled by oppressors. Not just theirs, but ours too. "The only thing necessary for the triumph of evil is for good men to do nothing" (Edmund Burke).

> Pray this prayer: *"Father in heaven, make me like the persistent widow, and give me victory in prayer with God, but also in court with judges. In Jesus' name, amen."*

> Assignment: *Call a Christian law firm in your area, especially one referred by Alliance Defending Freedom network, and schedule a consultation to discuss your case or issue, or invite them to speak to your crowd.*

> Get Credit: *Write 25 to 40 words engaging with ideas in this chapter and e-mail them to* homework@ schoolofliberty.org *under the email subject "Liberate Chapter 19."*

> *If you engage with all 30 chapters, we'll make you a "Certified Liberty Instructor." You might earn pay. Visit http://SchoolOfLiberty.org to learn more.*

WRITE YOUR PERSONAL NOTES AND QUESTIONS BELOW:

DAY 20

TOOL: RESOURCES
HOW TO RAISE MONEY

There are two kinds of politically active groups: the rich and powerful or the poor and oppressed. Personally, I love the oppressed; I believe God hears their prayers faster. But often God answers by using rich, powerful people to donate to the poor.

Because I want God to use me to help the poor, I've learned to ask the rich for money. I don't take a salary from my nonprofit, so it's easier to ask for donations when I know it's for the cause and not myself.

Raising money is a skill that requires humility, communications, and a big net. It's like fishing. You may target and net the occasional one-thousand-dollar donor, but I've had far greater success mobilizing crowds of smaller twenty-five-dollars donors. The more small donors you start with, the better chance one of them will give big later.

Donors give to passionate leaders. If your heart burns like fire for your cause, your vision catches on. Let your passion be visible and audible to donors. Donors also give to transparent, trustworthy, high-character leaders. If you're not one yet, work for one.

Best technique? Honestly, I'm no expert, so here's my advice: **Hire a professional fund-raising expert** with proven integrity. They're rare and hard to find, but when you find one, they'll teach you how to fish. If they require a small percentage of proceeds, they're worth it. But if they gouge your cause to enrich themselves, they're not worth it. Negotiate. Marketing campaign strategies vary, so try this:

1. Make sure your website has a *big* donate button and many options for payments, credit cards, PayPal, or other popular payment methods.
2. E-mail campaigns can be inexpensive, but less profitable when self-managed.
3. Direct postal mail can be expensive, but more profitable if run by a professional mail house.
4. Crowdfunding sites like Kickstarter, Indiegogo, and GoFundMe may go viral, but may not fit your cause. Compare by searching for "fund-raising sites."

File articles of incorporation for your nonprofit organization. Form a board, follow the law, and keep meticulous records for tax-deductible receipts for donors. Be totally transparent and honest with the public, and *never* defraud with dishonest claims. Then, if your cause is just and your people highly integral, don't be ashamed to ask, ask, ask for money. Go for it. If you're unselfishly helping the oppressed in Jesus' name, you also help your donors love their neighbor. I firmly believe givers earn points in heaven, so help your donors store treasure in heaven. Ask them to give.

Pray this prayer: *"Father in heaven, I trust You to be my provider, and I ask You to provide for me, my daily bread. Give me connections with like-minded donors who care about Your cause, and help me earn their trust. In Jesus' name, amen."*

Assignment: *Pray about your personal integrity limits in fund-raising techniques. What would violate your conscience? Never cross that line. Ask God to provide, describe your vision, then be assertive and ask.*

Get Credit: *Write 25 to 40 words engaging with ideas in this chapter and e-mail them to* homework@ schoolofliberty.org *under the email subject "Liberate Chapter 20."*

If you engage with all 30 chapters, we'll make you a "Certified Liberty Instructor." You might earn pay. Visit http://SchoolOfLiberty.org to learn more.

WRITE YOUR PERSONAL NOTES AND QUESTIONS BELOW:

VICTORY STORY

INDIANA COURT RESTORES JESUS PRAYERS

When anti-Jesus complainers didn't like hearing a pastor pray "in Jesus' name" before the legislature, they sued the Speaker of the Indiana state house Brian Bosma. The case came before a liberal judge David Hamilton, who ruled the word *Jesus* was illegal speech somehow banned by the First Amendment and that visiting pastors should be censored or disinvited as future prayer givers.

Strangely, Judge Hamilton ruled that prayers to *Allah* were perfectly acceptable, and only *Jesus* was banned as too sectarian. This is how he explained his ruling in *Hinrichs v. Bosma*:

> The injunction orders the Speaker . . . that the prayers should not use Christ's name or title or any other denominational appeal. . . . If those offering prayers in the Indiana House of Representatives choose to use the Arabic 'Allah'. . . the court sees little risk that the choice of language would advance a particular religion or disparage others.[12]

In other words, Christian speech is illegal, but Muslim speech is totally legal during a public prayer. Are you kidding me? When I read his crazy anti-Jesus ruling, I did not sit idly by. I took action.

Now I'm not a lawyer, I don't even play one on TV, but I know how to work the phones. I called some Christian lawyers at the Rutherford Institute who volunteered to help me advocate. They heroically submitted an amicus brief to the Indiana State attorney general, who appealed the case to the Seventh Circuit Court of Appeals. The brief incorporated many of our legal arguments demanding free speech.

We won, thank God, upon appeal, when the Seventh Circuit Court of Appeals in 2007 ruled 2-1 that Jesus prayers were allowed, and the anti-Jesus complainers did not have standing to sue because the First Amendment protects speech and religious expression even in public, and does *not* protect the easily offended ears of the anti-Jesus complainer. Speaker Bosma was vindicated, and pastors' liberty to pray "in Jesus' name" was restored in Indiana.

Sadly, when President Obama took office, one of the first judges he promoted to the Seventh Circuit was, you guessed it, the anti-Jesus Judge David Hamilton. But I made Hamilton's confirmation difficult. I wrote op-eds, contacted news reporters, e-mail blasted tens of thousands of Christians, and mobilized perhaps a half-million petitions to the U.S. Senate to oppose and filibuster Hamilton's confirmation. In the end he was confirmed, but barely, with only one Republican, from his home state, supporting Hamilton. Our public pressure delayed his confirmation for five months, and nearly caused the so-called nuclear option (to kill the U.S. Senate's ability to filibuster of judges), and broke the unity of the moderate "gang of fourteen" senators way back in 2009.

Bottom line: Judges are not above "we the people." One good cause led by one motivated activist leading a citizen "army" can upset an entire legislature. And even if you're not a lawyer, *you* can help others appeal bad rulings in court, and restore liberty!

Judge David Hamilton ruled you can pray to Allah but not "in Jesus' name" in Indiana

DAY 21

TOOL: GROUPS
JOIN LIKEMINDED GROUPS

The more the merrier. Your cause may be unique, but you are not alone in the fight for liberty. So many local county groups battle against big government that I'm very encouraged about our nation's future.

Your mission (should you choose to accept it) is to join as many excellent, local chapters of pro-liberty groups as you possibly have time for or money on which to spend.

Start at your political party headquarters. Ask them where and when conservative political groups meet every month. Your county probably already has some Tea Party, pro-gun, pro-faith, pro-liberty, pro-Israel, and conservative women's groups in many towns. By joining them you'll do two things: (1) Plug in to support what God's already doing through local people, and (2) find places and people who support your cause.

When I was a Navy chaplain, for example, fighting for my right and others' right to pray "in Jesus' name," I went to Washington, DC, and met with reps from thirty-five outside groups representing at least 70 million evangelical voters. They loved me. I stood for their favorite cause and let them use my story to excite their base of supporters. When 300,000 petitioners asked Congress to change the law, we won. I had no organization of my own, but I instantly found 70 million friends, by simply joining thirty-five national groups and meeting their leaders.

They raised money with my story, and I'm glad they did, because it made all of them stronger, which helped our common cause. I was their poster child, but it also raised my name recognition for the future.

Politically, I build bridges across theologies, so long as they fight for pro-liberty conservative ideals. While I am Pentecostal, for example, and I do not attend Mormon or Catholic church services, I happily join their pro-life cause and support for traditional marriage between one man and one woman. Personally, I do not align with totalitarian Muslims or Log-Cabin Republicans who politically oppose our religious liberty. Liberals oppose liberty, because ironically they prefer totalitarian big government and often hate social conservatives. This is why Democratic pro-abortion women and LGBT activists now march with Muslim men shouting "Allah Akbar" in the streets. I won't join them.

If you donate just ten dollars online to any group, you'll likely get on their e-mail list and mailing list forever. It's worth it, even if you never give again. Create a BACN folder to de-clutter your inbox, but don't unsubscribe. Instead automatically filter their e-mails to arrive in a folder which you may read someday. That way you can keep your inbox clear, but subscribe to as many newsletters as your political allies care to send you. Some of their "action alert" news sources will keep you better informed than major media. And you can study and follow their e-mail models before you e-blast your own list.

Pray this prayer: *"Father in heaven, I ask you to give me strategic alliances with like-minded liberty groups online and in my local community. In Jesus' name, amen."*

Assignment: *Subscribe to AFA.net, WND.com, The Blaze, Breitbart, Heritage.org, PrayInJesusName.org e-mail lists. Join your local pro-life, pro-faith, and pro-liberty political groups. Attend your party's meetings every time their door is open.*

Get Credit: *Write 25 to 40 words engaging with ideas in this chapter and e-mail them to* homework@ schoolofliberty.org *under the email subject "Liberate Chapter 21."*

If you engage with all 30 chapters, we'll make you a "Certified Liberty Instructor." You might earn pay. Visit http://SchoolOfLiberty.org to learn more.

WRITE YOUR PERSONAL NOTES AND QUESTIONS BELOW:

DAY 22

TOOL: LOCATION
SHOW UP TO YOUR STATE CAPITOL

As a former state representative having served in the Colorado legislature, I can honestly tell you that legislators respect, even fear, those who show up in person. *Politicians don't listen to silent or absent people.*

If you completed your assignment from Day 18, you have researched your legislators' calendar of committee hearings for your favorite issue. Maybe it's a pro-life bill coming up for a vote, a pro-home-schooling rally at the capitol, or some religious freedom that is under attack. You've asked your legislator's aide for instructions and prepared to testify at committee. Now go!

Invite two or three friends, and schedule the day together. Bring young people so they can watch. Your activism at the state capitol can inspire generations! Print any handouts you wish to give legislators. Get in the same car together, map out your parking space, and arrive early to pray at the capitol. Find your legislator's office and introduce yourselves to their aides. Then find the committee room and sign the roster of those who may testify. Ask the clerk or sergeant-at-arms when you're scheduled to speak. Mentally prepare your brief remarks, either for or against the issue or bill.

Ask the Lord to guide your words. He will speak through you. "When you are brought before synagogues, rulers and authorities, do not worry about how you will defend yourselves or what you will say, for the Holy Spirit will teach you at that time what you should say" (Luke 12:11–12).

Fear not! You follow the example of the Old Testament prophets who spoke God's Word to kings and often suffered for their faith. We don't suffer much today, comparatively, so again, fear not.

The worst likely outcome is unkind legislators may ask tough questions or ignore you before voting against you. Their comments or votes actually give useful information, since a no vote against God's morality or a yes vote for immorality can be used to campaign against them in the next election. Take notes and record their quotes. Publish a record by e-mail blast to your crowd. Include the phone numbers of legislators to thank or pressure. Expose evil; promote good.

The best likely outcome is that legislators listen attentively, ask you easy questions, and vote yes for godly morality, making laws that establish God's kingdom of love and justice on this earth. After the meeting, design sample postcards that might be mailed to voters during the next election cycle. "Did you know your legislator said _____ and voted for (or opposed) _____?"

Pray this prayer: *"Father in heaven, give me access to key brokers in the halls of power at my state capitol. Give me courage to speak truth to power. In Jesus' name, amen."*

Assignment: *Create a Facebook event page for your small group. Invite friends to join you at the capitol for a specific committee hearing about your issue. Recruit like-minded people to join you. If you cause a crowd to show up, you can whip the vote and win legislators.*

Get Credit: *Write 25 to 40 words engaging with ideas in this chapter and e-mail them to* homework@ schoolofliberty.org *under the email subject "Liberate Chapter 22."*

If you engage with all 30 chapters, we'll make you a "Certified Liberty Instructor." You might earn pay. Visit http://SchoolOfLiberty.org to learn more.

WRITE YOUR PERSONAL NOTES AND QUESTIONS BELOW:

VICTORY STORY

SUPREME COURT RULES JESUS PRAYERS OK

Even in liberal Democrat states like New York, conservatives can win through persistence. One day I read of a potential controversy in the town of Greece, New York, where heroic Supervisor John Auberger allowed pastors to pray "in Jesus' name" before council meetings. Anti-Jesus complainers with Americans United for the Separation of Church and State wrote a demand letter and hinted they'd sue.

I immediately faxed a two-page letter to Auberger, (which is published here: http://bit.ly/ChapsGreece) in which I encouraged him to hire some Christian lawyers with Alliance Defending Freedom (ADF). They published a model policy to allow Jesus prayers, and would defend those attacked pro bono in court. I never heard back from Auberger. I didn't do anything else but try to start that ball rolling and pray.

But soon I read Auberger adopted elements of ADF's pro-Jesus policy, and hired the same lawyers I had recommended. To ensure diversity, the court acknowledged a "Wiccan priestess and the chairman of the local Baha'i congregation each delivered one of these prayers, and a lay Jewish man delivered the remaining two," but the vast majority of 120 prayers were Christian.[13] I applaud this diversity because it is biblical. Elijah encouraged others to " 'call on the name of your god, and I will call on the name of the LORD. The god who answers by fire—he is God.' Then all the people said, 'What you say is good' " (1 Kings 18:24). This diversity allows freedom, not conformity.

What unfolded became our greatest legal victory imaginable, but not before a setback. As I predicted, the anti-Jesus complainers sued and lost in district court in 2010. But they appealed and won 3-0 at the Second Circuit Court of Appeals in 2012. Then Auberger appealed to the U.S. Supreme Court, and Greece beat the atheists.

In a 5-4 split decision that forever allowed Americans to pray publicly "in Jesus' name" the U.S. Supreme Court ruled in 2014 in the case of *Greece v. Galloway*:

> The prayers delivered in the town of Greece do not fall outside the tradition this Court has recognized. A number of the prayers did invoke the name of Jesus, the Heavenly Father, or the Holy Spirit, but they also invoked universal themes, as by celebrating the changing of the

seasons or calling for a 'spirit of cooperation' among town leaders…the Constitution does not require it to search beyond its borders for non-Christian prayer givers in an effort to achieve religious balancing."[14] (Read the full Supreme Court ruling here: http://bit.ly/GreeceGalloway).

Bottom line: Even if you're not a lawyer, just an ordinary activist, *you* can pick up the phone or write a letter to build a team that will grow over time, and win real, permanent victories for liberty, all the way to the Supreme Court. You can help make history!

*Supervisor John Auberger fought for liberty and won
5-4 at the U.S. Supreme Court*

DAY 23

TOOL: EXPERIENCE
BECOME AN INTERN, AIDE, OR STAFFER

Your legislator needs help at the office and hires local talent to answer the phones, draft letters or e-mails, negotiate deals, prepare bills, or help citizens. If you want to be effective and learn the process, volunteer as a legislative aide. This job experience will teach you better than any book or school how laws are made, and how to liberate the world.

One key to earning your legislator's trust or getting hired as an intern, aide, or staffer is to first help your legislator win reelection by volunteering on their campaign, which I'll discuss in Day 25. If you are hired, remember professional relationships are built over time, and your responsibilities and pay may grow the longer you serve, but **loyalty** is the currency of politics. If you are loyal, you'll be trusted. Jesus said, "You have been faithful with a few things; I will put you in charge of many things" (Matt. 25:23).

A successful aide *never says no* to a constituent, and never makes promises on behalf of a legislator. It's the boss's job to commit themselves, not yours. Practice phrases like, "I will record your request and pass it along to the representative." But never offend a citizen voter, because ultimately *they* are the boss over every elected official at election time. "Nor should there be obscenity, foolish talk or coarse joking, which are out of place" (Eph. 5:4).

An aide's loyalty should extend three ways: To your legislator, to his team, and to their issue or cause. When loyalties conflict too greatly, your resignation is better than your sabotage. Never, never, never stab your own boss or team in the back, or your reputation will be ruined and your career will end.

The most respected legislator I personally know was first a thirty-year military veteran, retired Air Force colonel, who sought a second career in politics. With humility he started out working as an unpaid intern, answering phones, for his own state legislator. After he learned the ropes, he waited for an opening and ran for office himself. He is now the top-ranking senator and chairman of the state's Joint Budget Committee, perhaps the most powerful leader in the legislature. He started out answering phones.

Half the legislators I know are former aides or volunteers. Let that sink into your mind. Half of those who win elections got their start helping an elected official, usually by starting without pay. Your investment to receive on-the-job training from a legislator dramatically increases your odds of someday learning how to run and win a seat yourself.

Pray this prayer: *"Father in heaven, give me access to one special legislator that I can serve as an intern at the capitol, and help me be loyal to serve them, even as Elisha served Elijah, until someday I receive their mantle. In Jesus' name, amen."*

Assignment: *Call the offices of three local elected officials and request to meet each of them one on one for coffee. Give them a copy of your résumé and say you want to work for them part time, without pay. Prepare to be surprised when one accepts your offer.*

Get Credit: *Write 25 to 40 words engaging with ideas in this chapter and e-mail them to* homework@ schoolofliberty.org *under the email subject "Liberate Chapter 23."*

If you engage with all 30 chapters, we'll make you a "Certified Liberty Instructor." You might earn pay. Visit http://SchoolOfLiberty.org to learn more.

WRITE YOUR PERSONAL NOTES AND QUESTIONS BELOW:

DAY 24

TOOL: PARTY
JOIN A POLITICAL PARTY

I f you've read this book this far, you're likely already registered to vote with some political party. For most Bible-believing Christians that's likely Republican, Libertarian, Constitution, Conservative, or America's Party. I will not tell you in this book, which party you should join. But there's *so* much more to joining a party than registering.

I mean really *join* the party. Parties are fun! They often involve better competition than sports. Get involved by attending every meeting you can. Fully fighting for your party platform is exhilarating.

Theodore Roosevelt said in 1910:

> It is not the critic who counts; not the man who points out how the strong man stumbles, or where the doer of deeds could have done them better. The credit belongs to the man who is actually in the arena, whose face is marred by dust and sweat and blood; who strives valiantly; who errs, who

comes short again and again, because there is no effort without error and shortcoming; but who does actually strive to do the deeds; who knows great enthusiasms, the great devotions; who spends himself in a worthy cause; who at the best knows in the end the triumph of high achievement, and who at the worst, if he fails, at least fails while daring greatly, so that his place shall never be with those cold and timid souls who neither know victory nor defeat.[15]

Wow! Memorize that quote.

Power goes to people who show up. My life as an activist and former elected official proves that. In politics, the teams that win are the ones with more people on them than the other side. I owe a great debt to every volunteer, donor, vendor, telephone caller, door knocker, and prayer warrior who loved their country enough to fight by my side. Our team needs you! So put on thick skin and *prepare to feel the emotions of battle.*

Join a party, but do not run for office right away. Have no agenda but to help serve others and be friendly. At first people will suspect your motives. (Why do you always show up?) Be transparent and soon the party faithful will trust you.

Do not run for office until you have volunteered helping at least three to five other local county campaigns without pay. Memorize the names and faces of others who show up often. Have coffee privately with each activist in your county party. Learn who are friends and who are enemies. Discover whom you can really trust to keep their word, and never lie or break your promises. Pick good mentors or coaches and ask them to teach you. Lay the groundwork for your own future race. Suddenly when you're not looking, people will ask you to run for something. *Still say no.* Pray, pray, pray, and when God and your family say yes, you'll be ready.

Pray this prayer: *"Father in heaven, I pray for wisdom on which political party I should join to be most effective for Your kingdom. None are perfect, but I pray you can make me salt and light within an imperfect party, to restore liberty. In Jesus' name, amen."*

Assignment: *Go spend a few hours at your local county party headquarters, learning who's who. Then commit to attending and volunteering, every time their door is open.*

Get Credit: *Write 25 to 40 words engaging with ideas in this chapter and e-mail them to* homework@ schoolofliberty.org *under the email subject "Liberate Chapter 24."*

If you engage with all 30 chapters, we'll make you a "Certified Liberty Instructor." You might earn pay. Visit http://SchoolOfLiberty.org to learn more.

WRITE YOUR PERSONAL NOTES AND QUESTIONS BELOW:

VICTORY STORY

CONGRESS GETS RELIGION AT PENTAGON

When anti-Jesus complainers like Mikey Weinstein, Americans United, Freedom from Religion Foundation, the ACLU, and others complain that American service members must not express their Christian faith in public or in uniform, confused commanders write bad policies. For example, Air Force Instruction 1-1 once prohibited Air Force officers from talking about their personal religious beliefs. Court-martials were threatened, so we took action to amend it.

After Phil Sheldon helped me send five million fax petitions to Congress, they twice in 2013 and 2014 added pro-faith amendments to the NDAA (National Defense Authorization Act, the law funding the military), restoring and strengthening religious liberty for our troops. When the liberal media wouldn't cover this, we became the media and hosted Congressman John Fleming on our national TV show. Fleming explained:

> There seems to be a sense among liberals in Washington, and even some of those in the

military, that the only way you can allow people to be openly gay or even have gay marriage, is somehow you have to stifle religious liberty, and particularly the liberty of expression. And not just for Christians, but for other forms of rights or beliefs of conscience. And so that's been sort of a battle that's been ongoing.[16]

His Fleming Amendment became law, and the formerly anti-Jesus AFI 1-1 was revised to say:

Every Airman also has the right to individual expressions of sincerely held beliefs, to include conscience, moral principles or religious beliefs...if it is necessary to deny free exercise of religion...it must directly relate to the compelling government interest of military readiness, unit cohesion, good order, discipline, health, safety, or mission accomplishment, and must be by the least restrictive means necessary to avoid the cited adverse impact.[17]

Jesus won. But more broadly, over the years we've partnered with bigger ministries who earned many more followers and had a greater impact than I, including Family Research Council, Christian Coalition, Faith and Freedom Coalition, American Family Association, Focus on the Family Action, Vision America, Foundation for Moral Law, Concerned Women for

America, Alan Keyes' Loyal to Liberty, America's Party, the American Center for Law and Justice, Liberty Counsel, First Liberty Institute, Alliance Defending Freedom, Heritage Action, Faith 2 Action, Faith and Action, Priests for Life, American Right to Life, and countless citizen volunteers who (1) sign petitions, (2) make phone calls, and (3) win elections. These activist groups deserve great credit for all they do (and you do by supporting them) as they daily defend liberty.

We are indebted to and grateful for all of you who have helped any pro-faith congressman get elected. Thank you for your hours of phone calls and door knocking, and for posting yard signs and giving donations. Because of you chaplains and troops have religious freedom for themselves, just like they sacrifice to defend for us.

More Info at www.PrayInJesusName.org

Congressman John Fleming defends liberty and appears on Chaps' TV show PIJN NEWS

DAY 25

TOOL: CAMPAIGN
HELP A CANDIDATE

No candidate is fully like Jesus. But we've got to find and support those who come as close as possible. That means first understanding who Jesus is, and what He believes by reading Matthew, Mark, Luke, and John. Then it means understanding His kingdom and His mandate that we liberate the world.

In a democratic republic like ours, power goes to elected officials who run for office and win votes. They make laws and enforce laws that promote either liberty or tyranny. This is a political reality in our modern world, and if we want laws that protect our religious freedom, we must help elect Christian candidates. The alternative is, we will be ruled by evildoers who impose tyranny and destroy freedom.

Finding candidates is not difficult. Just go to your party headquarters and ask who's running. But finding *good* candidates is very difficult, and that requires interviewing each candidate in person, face to face, to quiz them deeply about their beliefs and values. If they refuse to meet you, or do not share your biblical values, they are not worth volunteering your precious hours to help. But if they do share your views, help them. If they do not, actively expose and oppose them.

Candidates need a team of activists to win a local election. You are now an activist; you have a growing army of followers, and you have credibility within your circle of influence. Use that to help your favorite Christian candidate, as follows:

1. Publish your statement of endorsement for your candidate, in your personal capacity (not as leader of your organization), on your social media/email blast.

2. Personally donate the maximum allowable amount to your candidate's official campaign committee, but do not expect a tax-deduction.

3. Ask your followers to donate money to your candidate and raise money for election.

4. Show up at town-hall meetings where they speak, and volunteer to work their registration/book table.

5. Volunteer to make telephone calls to other activists in their district, the sooner the better. Don't wait for election day, start the snowball effect early.

6. Volunteer to pound yard-signs on high-traffic corners (not just your yard) to raise their "name ID" recognition in the district. Unknowns don't win.

7. Volunteer to make telephone calls to actual voters in the months leading up to election day. Your candidate can get voter rosters from the county clerk.

8. Volunteer to knock on at least 100 or 1,000 doors in person each weekend or weeknight to distribute their literature and have conversations on porches. Most voters never go to meetings, but they're home and willing to talk.

Pray this prayer: *"Father in heaven, lead me to support the right candidates for public office, and help them live up to your standards, especially if they win office. God prevent me from supporting candidates that will compromise godly principles or selfishly oppose Your Kingdom. Give us wisdom. In Jesus' name, amen."*

Assignment: *Ask to meet several candidates for coffee, see if they share your values, and ask how they need your help to get them elected. Your hours are worth more than cash.*

<u>Get Credit</u>: *Write 25 to 40 words engaging with ideas in this chapter and e-mail them to* homework@ schoolofliberty.org *under the email subject "Liberate Chapter 25."*

If you engage with all 30 chapters, we'll make you a "Certified Liberty Instructor." You might earn pay. Visit http://SchoolOfLiberty.org to learn more.

WRITE YOUR PERSONAL NOTES AND QUESTIONS BELOW:

TOOL: CANDIDACY
RUN FOR PUBLIC OFFICE

I f you have helped three to five candidates and attended candidate training via LeadershipInstitute.org, you have enough experience to run for office. If you feel called by God and your family supports it, look for a low-level race you can actually win, like school board, city council, county commissioner, state house. Unless you're a billionaire with unusually high name recognition, don't run for President first time out. Start small.

Pick your district carefully. If you live in a Democratic stronghold, run to build future traction, but don't expect to win the general election without a miracle. If you live in a Republican stronghold, fight tooth and nail to beat the RINO (Republican in Name Only) in the primary. Never challenge or oppose good people. If a real conservative Bible-believer holds office, support their reelection. Don't run against them. But if you feel called to challenge a liberal Pharisee, start early and hit 'em hard.

If you live in a moderate district that flops back and forth, tread carefully with your public statements and beware of the press. Always tell the truth and be positive and hopeful. Jesus said, "I am sending you out like sheep among wolves. Therefore be as shrewd as snakes and as innocent as doves" (Matt 10:16).

Do not announce you're a candidate until the right moment, politically. State laws often require formal written registration with the secretary of state the moment you publicly state you're a candidate. Memorize the legal requirements in your state regarding registering an official campaign committee with treasurer and bank account. Do not ignore them. Obey campaign finance laws that require periodic disclosure of every donor and expenditure. Find an experienced bookkeeper to handle your team's finances, write checks, pay bills, and file reports. Be transparent, and never allow your team to mismanage campaign funds for personal use.

Hire a campaign manager you trust, and pay them what they are worth. For a small race, budget at least five hundred to one thousand dollars per month for their salary. Hire an inexperienced, competent, motivated friend instead of an experienced stranger, because they'll control your life. As your career progresses you will make friends with experienced strategists you will someday trust and afford. If they can raise money or win elections with integrity, they are worth their fee. If you're going to run a big race for Congress, expect to pay a full-time wage for an experienced campaign manager. Research how much money past winners raised and spent, and follow their budget pattern for e-mail, radio, TV, postcards, and social media ads.

Pray this prayer: *"Father in heaven, only you know if I'm really called to become a candidate for public office. I want your best plan for my life, not my own. If public service is something you're calling me to, I ask you to make it very clear. God help me find and follow your calling on my life, not my own. In Jesus' name, amen."*

Assignment: *Pray about, and talk to your family about becoming a candidate.* **Candidates have only two jobs:** *Raise money and meet voters. Commit to dialing for dollars every day, spending hours on the phone asking for money. Attending meetings is not enough. To win you must knock on more doors than your opponent, period.*

Get Credit: *Write 25 to 40 words engaging with ideas in this chapter and e-mail them to* homework@ schoolofliberty.org *under the email subject "Liberate Chapter 26."*

If you engage with all 30 chapters, we'll make you a "Certified Liberty Instructor." You might earn pay. Visit http://SchoolOfLiberty.org to learn more.

WRITE YOUR PERSONAL NOTES AND QUESTIONS BELOW:

VICTORY STORY

FORMER NAVY CHAPLAIN
WINS ELECTION

If you are called by God, supported by family, and work to earn the support of volunteers, donors, and voters, you can rule liberate the world, or at least your small part of it, by winning election to public office. I did by serving in the Colorado state legislature.

Following is an excerpt of a WND article by Michael Carl on about my election victory:

> A former Navy chaplain who made headlines for being court martialed for praying in Jesus' name has been elected to the Colorado State House of Representatives.
>
> Former Chaplain Gordon Klingenschmitt, nicknamed "Chaps," won the seat Tuesday in Colorado House District with more than 70 percent of the vote.
>
> His work will begin in January.

"The Republicans increased their majority in both houses by one seat each. However, there is a Democratic governor. So the challenge will be to send good bills to the governor, even if he threatens to veto them," Klingenschmitt told WND.

He said his large margin of victory was because of the type of campaign he ran.

"I ran a positive, grassroots, door-to-door campaign. Volunteers went door-to-door, and I had 20 coffee events where I met the people face-to-face. The voters had a chance to meet me in person and find out that I'm a real person who is interested in their issues.

"At the same time, I declined several media interviews. I didn't want to conduct the campaign through the media. There were some good honest reporters, but most of the campaign was on the personal level," Klingenschmitt said.

Overall he says the election was about the principles of liberty.

"My supporters were all people who believe in the Constitution, liberty, freedom and small government. That's what the major national election was about. The people spoke and said they're for smaller government and more liberty," Klingenschmitt said.

He believes his election in Colorado was a reflection of the national mood.

"If you look at who won nationwide, the election was a statement against the attacks on religious liberty. It was a stand against courts on abortion, gay marriage," he said.[18]

(Read full story here: http://bit.ly/ChapsElected)

At this point I must publicly thank wife, Mary, my campaign manager, Patrick McGuire, his wife, Cyndi, and the one hundred plus volunteers who knocked on doors or made phone calls to help me win this race. In humility I must admit that later, after serving two years in the state house, I lost my bid for state senate. But win or lose, I always felt I was obeying God's call on my life.

My point in sharing this, and many other victories, is not to boast, but hopefully to inspire you. *You* can do everything I have done. *You* can run for public office and win. It's not easy, but it's also not rocket science. The fact you've read this far in my book proves

God is calling you to win. But if we don't win, Jesus is already King. Let's occupy until he comes.

Chaps Klingenschmitt wins election to Colorado legislature thanks to many volunteers

TOOL: MULTIPLY YOUR LABOR BUILD A TEAM OF VOLUNTEERS

Winning a political campaign requires building popular momentum. Like a small snowball rolling downhill, it gains traction and becomes an avalanche, an unstoppable force. Jesus said, "If you have faith as small as a mustard seed, you can say to this mountain, 'Move from here to there,' and it will move. Nothing will be impossible for you" (Matt. 17:20).

Faith requires believing strongly in your God, His calling, His kingdom, and your mission and purpose for running for political office. If you know why you're running, you will craft an inspiring message. That inspiring message is everything in politics. People are longing, even aching, for leadership that will solve their problems, and they will follow you and working tirelessly without pay to help you win.

Volunteers are the gasoline that fuels your momentum. One tireless volunteer is worth more than thousands of dollars in donations. Have coffee with them, tell them your inspiring vision, and give them direct access to your cell phone. **You, the candidate, must be your own volunteer manager.**

I won my first race for political office to the state legislature almost entirely because of my volunteers. I personally recruited and trained perhaps fifty local volunteers, mostly strangers who became dear friends, to knock on doors. They went door to door to reach thousands of voters, or worked the phones to earn votes. We were outspent by a rich candidate who bought much advertising with his own money, but he had almost no volunteers. We beat him by word-of-mouth, door-to-door marketing. We had conversations with voters on their porches. This required *starting early* and building momentum. Your personal army grows over time.

I lost my second race for political office to state senate in large part because seven outside groups spent perhaps a quarter million dollars in mostly false, nasty advertising. They sent anonymous postcards against me in the final month. If they're going to buy the race and are willing to lie, there's little you can do. But in the yearlong campaign I remained positive. I told the truth and compared voting records without false smears. I was proud to earn one hundred grassroots volunteers by my side (he had ten), knocking on doors and making phone calls. He had a couple millionaires writing anonymous checks through soft money, but I earned hundreds of small donors' trust. We nearly equaled their hard money. I lost that race, and

I blame only myself. But my friendships built with that team will last a lifetime. I owe them.

My point here is win or lose, you are building the kingdom of God. Who knows if those volunteers will run for office someday (two of mine already have), but if you show your followers true integrity, they'll follow your example.

Pray this prayer: *"Father in heaven, I pray you will help me teach good volunteers to take back their community, not for my own kingdom, but for Yours. God help me inspire the next generation of volunteer activists to win elections. In Jesus' name, amen."*

Assignment: *Find a creative way to thank or honor each unique person who has volunteered for you. Write and sign thank you notes, by hand, for each key volunteer.*

Get Credit: *Write 25 to 40 words engaging with ideas in this chapter and e-mail them to* homework@ schoolofliberty.org *under the email subject "Liberate Chapter 27."*

If you engage with all 30 chapters, we'll make you a "Certified Liberty Instructor." You might earn pay. Visit http://SchoolOfLiberty.org to learn more.

WRITE YOUR PERSONAL NOTES AND QUESTIONS BELOW:

DAY 28

TOOL: ALLIANCES
BUILD COALITIONS

I f you're like me, you care deeply and passionately about one particular issue that first inspired you to run an issue-based campaign. For me it was religious freedom and the right to pray "in Jesus' name." But running for public office is not about one issue, it is about dozens of issues your voters care about. You must learn all their issues.

Eventually you will become an expert in so many issues of public importance, but until then, join their issue teams and carry their torches as your own. Attend the meetings of all local pro-life groups. Sign up for e-mail lists of all local pro-family groups. Visit the churches of all politically minded pastors. Worship with them; get to know them personally. Attend the home-school convention and meet their pro-education lobbyist. Join the local gun club and attend all local Second Amendment meetings. Find the low-tax group and help them run issue campaigns. Find the pro-agriculture and pro-energy lobbyists, and ask them to explain their issues to you. *Listen.*

Find the pro-business political groups and the retired military veterans communities. Meet each of their leaders personally for coffee or by phone. They may or may not invite you to speak at their events, but you should join their cause to help them win, not always to help yourself. Let yourself be converted to their cause, if it is biblically aligned. When their leaders see you actually care, you'll earn their trust because you understand their issue. Once you earn their trust, you can earn their support, and maybe endorsement. With their endorsement comes their crowd, endless e-mail communications, positive social media posts, likely donations, more volunteers, and suddenly you've multiplied your base by joining forces.

Coalitions of different but parallel issue groups who have aligned for the sake of political survival can turn your snowball into their avalanche. The left has these coalitions too. They raise money and volunteer for candidates who will pass laws to promote their left-wing agenda, which is often anti-business, anti-energy, anti-farmer, pro-tax and spend, pro-union, pro-abortion, pro-LGBT, anti-church, anti-school choice, anti-gun, and anti-religious freedom. Their candidates succeed because their coalitions merge all these causes together, even if individuals started out caring for only one issue in particular.

Coalitions with fellow party members, in my case Republicans, are also valuable, but beware some "teammates" who actually intend to fight against your issue. Some Republicans may come to your coalition for their own reason but will differ from you on yours. They may even hate social conservatives and stab you in the back. Don't trust everyone until you verify their motives.

Pray this prayer: *"Father in heaven, help me build coalitions with people who may not share my priorities, but at least share my love for liberty. Give me powerful alliances with other coalitions within the conservative movement. In Jesus' name, amen."*

Assignment: *Make a list of all local groups, even those not affiliated with your cause.*

Get Credit: *Write 25 to 40 words engaging with ideas in this chapter and e-mail them to* homework@ schoolofliberty.org *under the email subject "Liberate Chapter 28."*

If you engage with all 30 chapters, we'll make you a "Certified Liberty Instructor." You might earn pay. Visit http://SchoolOfLiberty.org to learn more.

WRITE YOUR PERSONAL NOTES AND QUESTIONS BELOW:

VICTORY STORY

NEW LEGISLATOR REVERSES JESUS BAN

As a new legislator, I was sworn in with my right hand on the Bible, and took the oath to defend the Constitution. I was so excited, surrounded by friends and other legislators in the beautiful and historic state house of the Colorado capitol. I devoted my life to fully serving my constituents who had entrusted me as their representative.

Imagine my surprise when, after having helped change bad prayer policies in so many other states, I was told that my pastor would not be allowed to pray "in Jesus' name" if he said the invocation prayer on the floor of my own Colorado state house. I was shocked.

Pastors who were invited to pray received an official letter from a house committee which said in part, "Due to the religious diversity of our membership and because we ask that you not address any political issues, please keep your prayer or thought for the day non-sectarian and non-political so that all of those present may benefit from your words." In other words, you can pray to God but don't pray "in Jesus' name."

I knew what I must do. Once again I took a stand. Armed with a new ruling by the U.S. Supreme Court in Greece vs. Galloway, which clearly authorized pastors to pray publicly "in Jesus' name," even in a government forum, I went to the house clerk and showed her the case law precedent. I requested my pastor be allowed to pray "in Jesus' name," and I scheduled my pastor to come pray. But a confrontation was brewing.

The clerk emailed the Democrat speaker of the house, who told me she would be personally disappointed if my pastor prayed "in Jesus' name." But patiently I worked behind the scenes by talking to the house legal counsel, who admitted in a written memo that the previous anti-Jesus guidance was only a suggestion, and not binding.

"The relevant language is framed as a non-mandatory and thereby unenforceable request to visiting chaplains. . ." wrote Dan Cartin, the director of the Office of Legislative Legal Services, in a memo he sent to me, the house clerk, and the speaker. His memo conceded, no punishment could be enacted: "A chaplain's prayer has on occasion referenced Jesus Christ or another deity without consequence."

The Denver Post memorialized the events that followed:

Rep. Gordon Klingenschmitt. R-Colo. Springs, made his presence known in the House chamber . . . his supporting cast included the U.S. Supreme Court, his pastor and Jesus Christ.

The Rev. Mel Waters, an associate pastor of New Life Church in Colorado Springs, led the morning prayer in the House. He invoked the name of Jesus Christ. . .

Klingenschmitt sent a letter to House Speaker Dickey Lee Hullinghorst on Feb. 4 asking permission to invite his pastor to lead the morning prayer, and that Waters would conclude it, 'In Jesus' name we pray, amen.'

And that's what happened.[19]

(Read the full story, and watch me sing a Beatles' tune on the House floor here: http://bit.ly/ColoradoJesus).

Liberty won that day. My pastor prayed "in Jesus' name," without fear of consequence and with prior written permission. My activist career came full circle as I, with my pastor, helped restore the freedom to pray "in Jesus' name" in my home state legislature. I'm grateful to God we restored full liberty, which had been denied or at least threatened for some time before that day. Jesus won. *So can you.*

Colorado Pastor Mel Waters prayed "in Jesus' name" with State Rep. Klingenschmitt

TOOL: VICTORY
WHEN YOU WIN A POLITICAL RACE

t's Election Day, and you've won. Congratulations! If you've won a race as I have, remember after the election and before taking office, do these things:

1. Be humble. You won, but remember you're a servant leader, not a tyrannical ruler.
2. Be thankful. You owe a great debt to your volunteers and donors. Remain accessible to them by cell phone and find creative ways to thank each one.
3. Be gracious. If you won a close race, remember nearly half your constituents liked the other candidate better than they like you. Say nice things to news reporters about your opponent and try to mend any personal wounds you may have inflicted.
4. Prepare to study, study, study the office you're about to hold and the issues for

which you're about to do battle. You're no longer an outsider, you're an insider with clout.

Now the job of legislating or governing begins. After taking the oath of office, and for the next two or four years of your first term, do these things:

1. Learn the job. If you don't know something, ask an expert on the professional staff or administrator (or heaven forbid, ask a lobbyist) to give you needed knowledge. But realize they may also have agendas.

2. Build relationships on both sides, and be kind. Although I am ultra-conservative on social issues, I made it my personal mission to show unusual kindness to every left-wing Democrat I met. I never voted with them, but today they smile when they see me because they know I deeply cared for each one of them.

3. Hire your own office staff. Perhaps a few of your most loyal campaign volunteers are available to work as your paid or unpaid intern staff, but you also need to recruit some experienced experts to run an office. Usually an elected official will have an office budget that can pay staff. Loyalty

is premium. Never hire a backstabber or spy.

4. Train your own office staff. Teach them what you expect, even for seemingly mundane tasks like answering the phone. Tell them how they should "never say no to a constituent" but only take a message for you to read and consider, and above all be honest and cheerful.

5. Be loyal to **conscience** first, **constituents** second, **caucus** leaders third, and **coalitions** fourth. When conflicts arise and pressures are applied for your vote, follow God and conscience. Remember, you're building His kingdom first and not other peoples'.

My friend Tom Riner, a Christian Democratic legislator from Kentucky, once told me, "I vote for what God wants first. Then if it's not immoral then I vote how my constituents want." He served thirty-four years then lost for refusing to compromise Christian values.

Pray this prayer: *"Father in heaven, prepare my heart for victory by making me humble, so I am never corrupted by power, but empowered to love. In Jesus' name, amen."*

Assignment: *Join a weekly legislator prayer group or Bible study. If you can't find one, start one yourself.*

<u>Get Credit</u>: *Write 25 to 40 words engaging with ideas in this chapter and e-mail them to* homework@ schoolofliberty.org *under the email subject "Liberate Chapter 29."*

If you engage with all 30 chapters, we'll make you a "Certified Liberty Instructor." You might earn pay. Visit http://SchoolOfLiberty.org to learn more.

WRITE YOUR PERSONAL NOTES AND QUESTIONS BELOW:

DAY 30

TOOL: PERSEVERANCE
WHEN YOU LOSE A POLITICAL RACE

I am living proof, there is life after politics. If you've lost a race as I have, chalk it up as a learning experience. But don't quit. **You're not done with the fight.** You have valuable experience to mentor others who follow in your footsteps. Now teach others.

Take my humble attitude: If you win an election, it's only because others helped you, but if you lose, it was all your fault. While many factors cause wins and losses, the point here is not to blame your team. Take responsibility as humble leader of a lost mission.

Most of your team worked their tails off without pay to help you, and they deserve great amounts of praise and personal thanks, despite a loss. Losing an election stings, but your supporters love you and they feel the loss too. Tell press reporters how much you owe your supporters for how hard they worked.

Be gracious and call your opponent personally to concede immediately when it becomes clear it's over.

You'll be less bitter if you congratulate them quickly, and less jealous if you bless them—even if they cursed you. Compliment them for winning a hard-fought campaign. Don't take jabs or make snide remarks, even if you personally believe they did you wrong. Proverbs 25:21–22 says, "If your enemy is hungry, give him food to eat; if he is thirsty, give him water to drink. In doing this, you will heap burning coals on his head, and the Lord will reward you."

Pay your debts. Unpaid vendors put up their credit for your cause and must be paid in full, period. Whether you win or lose elections, keep your word. Spend time with your family. If you are blessed with a wife and children, recognize the sacrifice they made to allow you to pursue your dream. Reward them with personal attention. Take a vacation.

Do not question God's goodness. Here is the hardest lesson I've had to learn having tasted both sweet victory and a bitter election defeat: God is sovereign and smarter than we are. "As the heavens are higher than the earth, so are my ways higher than your ways and my thoughts than your thoughts," says the LORD in Isaiah 55:9. Thankfully, Christ already rules, so we don't always have to win.

Before I ran for State Senate in 2015–16, I prayed and fasted for three days for God's guidance. God spoke to me and brought tears to my eyes, promising, "I will give you every place where you set your foot" (Joshua 1:3), so I knocked on doors for months. But later in 2016, when secret dark-money operatives mailed tens of thousands of nasty, false, anonymous postcards against me, and falsely bought the election for my opponent and I lost, I questioned whether God called me to run in the first place. I was angry. But I forgave and chalked it up to a life lesson.

I concluded three things: (1) God is always good, (2) I was really called by God to run, and (3) God did not promise me victory but only reward if I were faithful in the attempt. Sometimes evil wins, but I know God will grant justice some day, in the end.

Pray this prayer: *"Father in heaven, even in defeat I trust and never doubt that you are a good God. Your ways are higher than my ways. Now help me teach others. Amen."*

Assignment: *Return to grateful worship, win or lose. Resolve to never quit. Teach others.*

Get Credit: *Write 25 to 40 words engaging with ideas in this chapter and e-mail them to* homework@ schoolofliberty.org *under the email subject "Liberate Chapter 30."*

If you engage with all 30 chapters, we'll make you a "Certified Liberty Instructor." You might earn pay. Visit http://SchoolOfLiberty.org to learn more.

WRITE YOUR PERSONAL NOTES AND QUESTIONS BELOW:

CONCLUSION

BUILDING THE KINGDOM OF GOD

We face competing kingdoms being built today by politically powerful adversaries that do not hold a Christian worldview, and they intend to rule us. If we do nothing, they will enslave us in totalitarianism, remove our Constitutional liberties, and ban our religious expression, forcing us to practice their beliefs or endure government punishment at their hands. I need not explain here the threats of Islamist political ideology. Many totalitarian Muslims understand dominion, and they are on a global march. They intend to rule us, unless we establish permanent liberty in our land.

If you think the American Left is sitting idly by or that the LGBT community wants peace and harmony with you, wake up. As a legislator I saw first hand just how well organized they are, and they intend to rule over us, already taking political dominion incrementally every day, not just for their own expression *but to forbid ours.* They say discrimination, but what they actually legislate is forced participation in sin.

If we fail to defend liberty, tyrants will rule us. Three times the government has punished me for praying in public or quoting the Bible in my own pulpit. Each time I fought back and demanded liberty. I learned the lessons of this book just to survive.

I teach these lessons to you at the little cost for this small book, but consider the great cost of our national survival if *you* do not implement them and share them!

Think about how many pastors or friends or acquaintances could use a copy of this book. Please give them a copy. Liberate the world, or be ruled by it.

Church arise!

ENDNOTES

1. "Congress directs Navy, Air Force to drop sectarian prayer ban," Christian Examiner, November 3, 2006, http://www. christianexaminer.com/article/congress-directs-navy-air-force-to-drop-sectarian-prayer-ban/43782.htm.

2. Read original documents including SECNAVINST 1730.7C, order by Navy Judge Lewis Booker, speech by Senator John Warner, and order by Congress and Navy Secretary rescinding 1730.7C at: http://prayinjesusname. org/about-chaps.

3. "There are 7 Mountains of Influence in Culture," 7 Cultural Mountains, Marketplace Leaders Ministries, accessed April 26, 2017, http://www.7culturalmountains.org.

4. Gordon Klingenschmitt, "Tulsa Welcomes Back Jesus," WND, March 1, 2008, http://www.wnd. com/2008/03/57668.

5. Matt Trewhella, "What is the Lesser Magistrate Doctrine?" Lesser Magistrate website, accessed April 26, 2017, http:// lessermagistrate.com/the-doctrine-of-the-lesser-magistrate/.

6. Erin James "State House edits 'Jesus' from pastor's prayer," Daily Record/Sunday News, July 22, 2009, http://ydr.inyork. com/ci_12683284.

7. Tom Barnes, "Pa. House Prayer Rejected over 'Jesus'," Pittsburgh Post-Gazette, July 19, 2009, http://www.post-gazette.com/news/state/2009/07/19/Pa-House-prayer-rejected-over-Jesus/stories/200907190234.

8. Charlie Butts, "Oregon City Council Keeps Prayer, Strikes 'non-sectarian'," OneNewsNow, July 28, 2008, http://www.

onenewsnow.com/politics-govt/2008/07/28/oregon-city-council-keeps-prayer-strikes-non-sectarian.

9. Gordon Klingenschmitt, "Anti-Jesus Activists on Warpath," WND, June 26, 2007, http://www.wnd. com/2007/06/42256/#x1x6OKlG34hExz5C.99.

10. Todd Starnes, "Pastor Yanked from Capitol over 'Jesus' Prayer," Fox News Radio, July 9, 2010, http://radio.foxnews. com/2010/07/09/pastor-banished-from-capitol-over-jesus-prayer/.

11. Ron Baity speech at a press conference, "Dr. Ron Baity Fired for Mentioning Jesus, Pt. 1," YouTube, August 4, 2010, http://www.youtube.com/watch?v=poFQiojHUxQ.

12. Hinrichs v. Bosma, Becket Religious Liberty for All, decision date: October 30, 2007, http://www.becketlaw.org/case/hinrichs-v-bosma/.

13. Galloway v. John Auberger, Find Law for Legal Professionals, May 17, 2012, http://caselaw.findlaw.com/us-2nd-circuit/1609945.html.

14. Greece v. Galloway, Supreme Court of the United States, May 5, 2014, http://www.supremecourt.gov/opinions/13pdf/12-696_bpm1.pdf.

15. Theodore Roosevelt, "The Man in the Arena," Citizenship in a Republic, April 23, 1910, http://www.theodore-roosevelt. com/trsorbonnespeech.html.

16. John Fleming, "Congressman John Fleming defends religious freedom for the troops," PIJN News, December 18, 2014, http://www.youtube.com/watch?v=py3ab4A2PHo.

17. "Air Force Standards, Air Force Culture," Air Force Instruction 1-1, Incorporating Change 1, November 12, 2014, http://static.e-publishing.af.mil/production/1/af_cc/publication/afi1-1/afi1-1.pdf.

18. Michael Carl, "Navy Chaplain who fought for Prayer Elected in Colorado," WND, November 8, 2014, http://

www.wnd.com/2014/11/navy-chaplain-who-fought-for-prayer-elected-in-colorado.

19. Joey Bunch, "Rep. Gordon Klingenschmitt brings Jesus one day, Beatles on another," *Denver Post*'s *The Spot* blog, February 27, 2015, http://blogs.denverpost.com/thespot/2015/02/27/rep-gordon-klingenschmitt-brings-jesus-one-day-beatles-another/117496/.

ABOUT THE AUTHOR

Chaplain Gordon James Klingenschmitt, PhD (aka "Dr. Chaps") is the national TV show host of PIJN NEWS, daily on the NRB-TV network on Direct TV Channel 378, and ten on-demand platforms, including Roku here: http://bit.ly/PIJNnews.

He is a former State Representative having won election to the Colorado legislature, affiliate faculty at Colorado Christian University, Air Force Academy graduate in Political Science, and made national headlines as the former Navy Chaplain who dared to pray "in Jesus' name." An ordained Pentecostal minister, he earned his PhD in Theology from Regent University and has been ranked among "the top 1% most endorsed in United States for Preaching" by Linkedin.

He is available as a motivational speaker, telling his inspiring true story of taking a stand for religious freedom by sacrificing a million dollar pension and demanding his own misdemeanor court-martial, then being vindicated by Congress who repealed the bad policy and restored the rights of all military chaplains to pray publicly "in Jesus' name."

His national petition organization, The Pray In Jesus Name Project, has delivered five million fax petitions to Congress, and overturned bad policies restoring religious liberty in thirteen states.

He may be contacted through his USA non-profit charity Pray In Jesus Name Ministries at 1-866-Obey-God, or invited to speak at chaps@schoolofliberty.org.

HOW YOU CAN HELP OUR CAUSE

Our cause is the cause of liberty. Part of our mission is to mentor the next generation of Christian political activists to take back their country and establish God's kingdom.

To donate tax-deductibly, please write to:
Pray In Jesus' Name Ministries
PO Box 77077
Colorado Springs, CO 80970

Subscribe to our free daily email alerts or watch our national TV show, PIJN News,
visit: http://prayinjesusname.org

Invite Gordon Klingenschmitt, PhD, to come speak to your crowd. E-mail: chaps@schoolofliberty.org
and put "Invitation for Chaps" in the subject line.

Become a "Certified Liberty Instructor!"
This devotional book is part of our easy, self-paced
30-lesson curriculum that we will license you to teach
your local small groups. Get credit by simply e-mailing us
one short essay after each chapter. Then access our videos
to show your class by joining our private, members-only
mentoring group: http://SchoolOfLiberty.org

SchoolOfLiberty.org

To order multiple copies or boxes of this book at a
bulk discount, call us toll-free at
1-866-Obey-God.

CPSIA information can be obtained
at www.ICGtesting.com
Printed in the USA
FSOW02n1409100917
38404FS